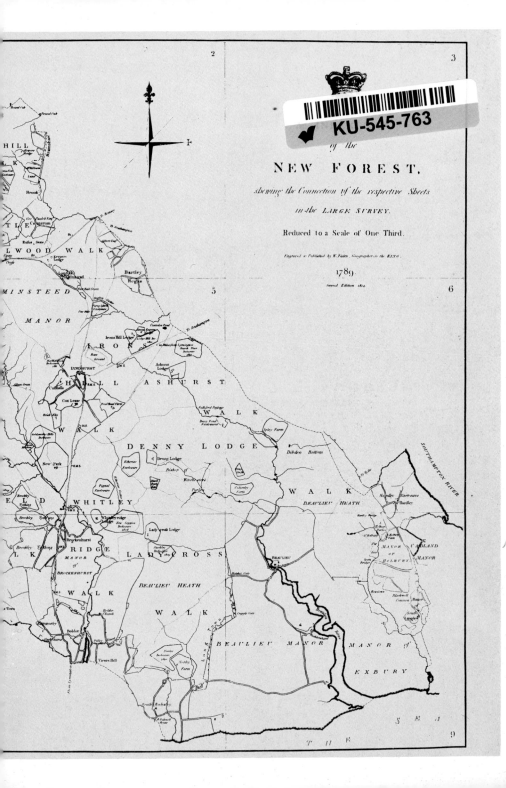

This book is designed to aid the reader's
enjoyment and knowledge of the
New Forest

London
Her Majesty's Stationery Office

Explore the New Forest

An official guide by the Forestry Commission

Edited by Donn Small, OBE and John Chapman

HMSO BOOKS

HMSO publications are available from:

HMSO Publications Centre
(Mail and telephone orders only)
PO Box 276, London, SW8 5DT
Telephone orders 01-873 9090
General enquiries 01-873 0011
(queuing system in operation for both numbers)

HMSO Bookshops
49 High Holborn, London, WC1V 6HB 01-873 0011 (Counter service only)
258 Broad Street, Birmingham, B1 2HE 021-643 3740
Southey House, 33 Wine Street, Bristol, BS1 2BQ (0272) 264306
9-21 Princess Street, Manchester, M60 8AS 061-834 7201
80 Chichester Street, Belfast, BT1 4JY (0232) 238451
71 Lothian Road, Edinburgh, EH3 9AZ 031-228 4181

HMSO's Accredited Agents
(see Yellow Pages)

and through good booksellers

Printed in the United Kingdom for Her Majesty's Stationery Office
Dd291278 C70 11/89

Front cover – *Bolderwood Walk*. [TH]
Back cover – *Fallow does in spring beechwood*. [TH]
Page 2 and 3:
Index to Drivers Map (see p. 46)
Page 4 and 5, left to right:
1 *Spring in oak plantations*. [HA]
2 *Summer in Holmsley Camp*. [RF]
3 *Autumn in Ancient and Ornamentals*. [HA]
4 *Winter on the heath*. [CP]

Contents

Foreword

Welcome to the New Forest

The Queen's House
Lyndhurst
Hampshire
SO4 7NH

The continuing popularity of this book amply supports the view of my predecessor Donn Small for the need to set out in a single attractive volume something of the background to the management of this unique area. The authors describe the history, wildlife and practical aspects of forest life making a splendid introduction to the Forest for visitors and indeed residents who wish to know more about it.

This new edition has provided an opportunity to update facts and information which I hope will assist those staying in or exploring the area.

The New Forest is ideal walking country and the visitor is welcome to walk on all the paths and tracks. The maps, each with a brief account of the area concerned, provide an excellent guide for the walker and indeed the motorist who wishes to savour something of the diverse character of the Forest.

For many the New Forest is an entirely engrossing experience, the source of endless pleasure and for very many visitors it can provide a place of relaxation, peace and even solitude in our overcrowded country. Much of this is a tribute to those who live and work in the Forest, those concerned with its sympathetic management and the many people who through their intense interest contribute to its care and survival.

David J. Perry
Deputy Surveyor
of the New Forest

2

1 *Bolderwood fallow deer in velvet.* [RF]
2 *Ancient and Ornamental woodlands.* [RF]
3 *Bolderwood Walk* [TH]
4 *Eyeworth Pond car park.* [FC]
5 *Ponies on Avon Water bank.* [RF]

4

3

5

Introduction

DONN SMALL

Historical background

When, about AD 1079, William I created his "New" Forest in this corner between the Solent and the sea, the land consisted of relatively infertile woodland and furzy waste, sparsely scattered with farms and homesteads. The act of afforestation in Norman times transformed a whole neighbourhood into a royal hunting preserve, placing it under the hated forest law, which involved the curtailment of liberty and drastic punishment meted out for any interference with the beasts of the chase or their haunts.

Since the unfortunate peasants who dwelt in the Forest were forbidden to enclose their land lest any fence should interfere with the free run of the deer, their domestic animals were allowed to graze by common right and browse throughout the Forest and this grazing, reinforced by that of the deer themselves, severely diminished the ability of the sparse woodlands to perpetuate themselves. The dearth of new trees became a serious problem during the middle ages, which saw an enormous increase in the consumption of wood, the principal raw material of the time, and enactments were made to enable large areas in the New Forest to be enclosed for the purpose of establishing woodlands, later to be thrown open when the trees were past the danger of damage by grazing animals. This process became known as the rolling power of enclosure. The first tree-growing act was passed in 1482

and others followed. The act of 1698 allowed the enclosure of 6 000 acres and as the Crown assumed rolling powers, this meant that the area of woodland could increase beyond that, to the detriment of the commoners' grazing rights.

With time the royal hunting rights became less important and there is no record of any sovereign hunting in the Forest after James II. The way was thus clear for the passing of the Deer Removal Act of 1851, under which the deer were ordered to be destroyed and in return the Crown were authorised to enclose and plant a further 10 000 acres. It subsequently proved impossible to remove the deer, but these new Inclosures aroused considerable opposition from the commoners, whose cattle still grazed the Open Forest. Followed a Select Committee investigation, the Act of 1877 was passed, under which the Crown gave up its rolling powers and no more land could be enclosed beyond what had been enclosed in the reign of William III and subsequently up to the passing of this Act. This amounted to nearly 18 000 acres, but the total area enclosed at any one time (other than the enclosure of Crown freehold land) might not exceed 16 000 acres. The Forestry Commission took over the management of the Forest in 1924 and the Act of 1949 authorised the enclosure of a further 5 000 acres, with the authority of the Verderers, for the growing of timber; just over 2 000 acres of this additional land has been enclosed and planted.

The New Forest today reflects the history of its woodlands and commons. The Timber Inclosures, some of which have been open for decades, with the Crown freeholds, take up less than a third of its area. The larger part is Open Forest, consisting of over 65 000 acres of grasslands, heath, scrub and the Ancient and Ornamental Woodlands, the ragged descendants of ancient Inclosures now developing as natural oak and beechwoods; the whole roamed by the commoners' animals – ponies, cattle, pigs – and the deer who have survived both the sport of kings and an Act of Parliament to exterminate them. The New Forest made a major contribution to the 1939-45 war, providing enough timber to build a bridge nine feet wide by 1½ inches thick from Southampton to New York from twenty six sawmills scattered throughout the woodlands. Remnants can still be seen today at Anderwood, Ashurst and Hawkhill. It was one of the largest assembly areas for the troops embarking on the invasion of France in 1944. Today visitation by the public exerts additional and a more rapidly destructive pressure on the Forest.

Geology and soils

The New Forest lies in a broad shallow basin – the Hampshire Basin – surrounded by the low chalk downlands of Cranborne Chase, the Wiltshire and Hampshire Downs, Ballard Down and the spine of the Isle of Wight. The basin is filled with gravels, sands and clays laid down when the Forest area was occupied by a large river estuary or shallow sea; the gravel was apparently spread over the previously-deposited clays and sands by glacial drift, forming gravel cappings which have been extensively eroded by streams to expose the underlying deposits below.

There are three main types of surface form: infertile, flat-topped gravel plateaux, rich well-drained clays and loams, and low-lying ill-drained marshland. The water-logging which characterises so much of the Forest is caused by the existence of a hard pan at a depth of one to three feet, or impervious clay beds, which account for the poverty of many of the Forest soils.

Vegetation

Three distinct types of vegetation are linked with the surface forms: heathland with self-sown Scots pine and birch, gorse, heather and hardy grasses; woodland on the long gentle slopes separating the plateaux – beech, oak, yew, holly and thorn; and on the marshy ground alder thickets, willows, heath, bracken, sedge, bog moss and cotton grass.

Conservation

Because the Forest is the home of so many rare plants, animals, reptiles, birds and insects, the Forestry Commission has signed a Minute of Intent with the Nature Conservancy Council recognising the Forest to be of National Nature Reserve status, and agreeing to consult with the Council on general policy with regard to the management of the Forest. The Commission has a statutory duty to drain the Open Forest and clear coarse herbage to protect the grazing for the Commoners' animals, and all plans for such work are agreed by joint committees on which the Nature Conservancy Council is represented. The Commission has put into effect a programme of conservation designed to protect the Forest against damage and penetration by tourists' cars with physical barriers to prevent car access, controlled camping areas, car parks, picnic places and other amenities which together will channel visitors to areas most able to accept them without major environmental degradation.

Page 10: *The Great Seal of William Rufus.*
Page 10 and 11: *The King Hunting.*

New Forest management plan

The overall management of the New Forest is the responsibility of the Forestry Commission, under the direction of the Deputy Surveyor of the New Forest, an ancient title for the officer in charge under the Surveyor General of all Crown forests. The latter appointment no longer exists. The agreed management plan for the period 1982–1991 is based on the Mandate presented at the Court of Verderers on 3 May 1971 by the Right Honourable James Prior MP, Minister of Agriculture, Fisheries and Food and has the following major objectives:

'The New Forest is to be regarded as a national heritage and priority given to the conservation of its traditional character.

The Ancient and Ornamental Woodlands are to be conserved without regard to timber production objectives.

In the Statutory Inclosures the existing balance between the conifers and broadleaves is to be maintained; the latter are to be managed with greater emphasis on visual amenity, on a rotation of at least 200 years and felling limited to single trees or small groups.'

The Statutory Inclosures, from which grazing animals are excluded by fences, contain a rich fauna and flora as well as mature trees, in contrast to the grazed open forest waste. By historical accident there is however an excess of mature broadleaved trees which if not regenerated would lead to an imbalance of age structure and their eventual decay. The objectives here are to achieve in the long term an even distribution of ages by regeneration treatments which will cause the minimum disturbance in the process, and in doing so to enrich the ecological diversity within each stand.

The Ancient and Ornamental Woodlands, which are not enclosed and are subject to deer browsing, grazing by commoners' animals and public recreation, consist chiefly of old oak and beech, probably the remnants of ancient plantings. A survey carried out in 1971 by the Forestry Commission has shown that 73 per cent of these woodlands contain an adequate naturally regenerated successor crop and that the total area of broadleaved forest has in fact increased since 1867 at an approximate rate of 12 acres per year. Artificial regeneration is therefore unnecessary but in some areas where the dominance of beech is likely to exclude future regeneration of oak, a continual and selective thinning of the beech to favour oak will be desirable to maintain an acceptable and enriched ecosystem.

The Open Forest Waste consists of natural heathland with gorse, areas artificially re-seeded with grass during the Second World War, self-seeded Scots pine, emerging Ancient and Ornamental Woodland and bog. An acceptable balance is to be kept between grazing for commoners' animals, biological diversity, stability of the surrounding woodland and peaceful enjoyment by the public. This will be achieved by rehabilitating heath and gorse for the purposes of rejuvenation, by not extending further artificially grass re-seeded areas and by carrying out drainage only to benefit the stability of surrounding woodland and the grazing, all without loss of biological diversity. Newly regenerating woodlands encroaching on the Forest Waste will be recruited to the Ancient Woodlands of the future. This will be done in consultation with

Open Forest
1 *Heathland, Latchmoor.* [DS]

Ancient and Ornamental
2 *Over mature and dying oak.* [DS]
3 *Beech natural regeneration.* [DS]

Statutory Inclosures
4 *Conifer artificial regeneration.* [DS]
5 *Oak artificial regeneration.* [DS]
6 *Beech natural regeneration.* [DS]

1

the Nature Conservancy Council and by agreement of the Verderers.

Recreational use of the Forest will be accommodated without allowing the Forest's fundamental character to change and with the minimum of conflict between the many diverse interests in the area. The provision of facilities designed and constructed by the Forestry Commission commenced in 1972 and is based upon the final recommendations of the Joint Steering Committee whose report was approved by the Minister of Agriculture in 1971.

These facilities consist of car parks and camping areas dispersed throughout the Forest in suitable locations, associated with areas protected from unofficial car access. The visitor is encouraged to walk into and learn from the Forest by the provision of waymarked walks and information services, including special facilities for educational use by schools; and there is co-ordination of specialised activities to avoid conflict with other uses of the Forest.

Involvement, understanding and encouragement by the visitor is essential if such major conservation measures are to be successfully completed. In 1971 the Forestry Commission formed the New Forest Consultative Panel, on which over 45 different bodies are represented and by which management and recreation proposals are discussed. This is in addition to the statutory agreement which must be obtained from the Verderers.

Constant monitoring is undertaken by the Forestry Commission to ensure that adequate measures can be embarked on to meet the enormous pressures that the Forest is subject to today.

The New Forest is probably unique in the world for its historical associations, its rare animals and plants and its living traditions. It lies within easy reach of millions of people and the Forestry Commission will ensure that in making the beauty of its wilderness freely available to them it also takes adequate precautions to see that it is not destroyed.

2

3

4

5

6

One

How the Forest has survived

DAVID J STAGG

"The forest law is hereby abrogated". These six words which are contained in the Wild Creatures and Forest Laws Act 1971 mark the formal ending of forest legislation dating back to at least the twelfth century. The majority of these laws had long become obsolescent, but at one time they were essential for the protection of the forest and the king's deer, and to a lesser extent to define and limit the duties and responsibilities of the inhabitants of the forest.

It is frequently stated that the forest laws were first introduced by King Canute, but this is untrue and the document upon which the claim is based has been proved to be a forgery. The forest laws were made by the Norman kings, the earliest surviving text being that known as the Assize of Woodstock and dated 1184, but this can be shown by documents of the period to be nothing more than a re-enactment and possible expansion of the then existing laws, and in fact the very first article refers to the more stringent penalties which had been exacted during the reign of Henry I.

The restrictions, which were intended to protect the game, included the possession of bows and arrows, the keeping of unlawed dogs – that is dogs not lamed so as to prevent them chasing the deer, the setting of traps for deer, and hunting at night. For the preservation of the woods it was an offence to cut timber except under the supervision of a forester, and far more serious was the offence of assarting – the conversion of woodland into arable land, and purprestures – the enclosing of forest land. More information is contained in a document known as "The Customs and Assise of the Forest". This details the customs and laws concerning trespasses to the vert and the venison, the procedure of the Courts, the duties of the inhabitants, and those of the foresters. For instance it gives such detail as the number of sureties in respect of various offences, these

being required to ensure the attendance of the offender at the next Forest Court. If a deer was found dead it was required that an inquest should be held among the four nearest villages.

The Charter of the Forest AD 1217, the forest's equivalent to Magna Carta, granted some relaxation of the forest laws. It was provided that certain recent extensions of the forests should be disafforested, an amnesty was granted to offenders who has been previously outlawed or exiled, fewer attendances were required at the Forest Courts, certain improvements to private lands within the forest would no longer be regarded as purprestures, rights of common were protected, there were to be safeguards against abuses and extortion by officials of the Crown, and no longer could offences be punished by mutilation or death.

The administration of justice within the forests was done in two stages, first by a local Court which determined whether an offence had been committed but was not empowered to pass sentence, the offenders being referred to the Forest Eyre, or Justice Seat, a Court presided over by the Lord Chief Justice in Eyre and held at irregular intervals around the various forests. The last such Court was held in the New Forest in 1669–70, and although the forest laws remained in force, the New Forest Act of 1698 specifically drawing at tention to this point – "the said Forest and every Part thereof shall be subject to and under the Laws of the Forests", the actual enforcement of these laws became virtually impossible.

The 1698 Act was primarily concerned with the establishment of timber Inclosures, but it did give the lesser Courts, held by the Verderers and known as the Court of Swainmote and the Court of Attachment, the power to impose fines for such offences as stealing timber, burning the heath, and destroying the covert. Further

ANNO NONO & DECIMO

GULIELMI III. REGIS.

C A P. XXXVI.

An Act for the Increase and Preservation of Timber in the *New Forest* in the County of *Southampton*.

powers were given by the New Forest Act 1800 in respect of unlawful enclosures, purprestures, and encroachments, and an Act of 1819 gave powers over the exercise of common rights, and the right to enquire into the conduct of the under-officers employed in the forest. Throughout this period it was also possible, if less convenient, for more serious offences to be dealt with by the Court of Assize at Winchester.

The greatest threat to the New Forest did not arise from minor encroachments and the destruction of timber, but occurred in 1871 when the Treasury introduced into Parliament a Bill for the Disafforestation of the New Forest. This was a course that had been adopted for other royal forests, but fortunately on this occasion public opinion was aroused and the Bill was withdrawn. Reaction went even further in that a Resolution was passed in the House of Commons that no felling of timber should take place, and no further timber Inclosures be made, pending legislation on the New Forest. This took the form of the New Forest Act 1877, which is still largely in force and forms the basis of modern day management of the Forest. Under this Act the

Crown's powers of Inclosure were greatly limited, and, equally important, amenity considerations were recognised in that regard was to be given to maintaining the picturesque character of the Forest, with attention being given to its ornamental value. The interpretation and implementation of this Act has from time to time aroused considerable controversy, especially so in the economic conflict between broadleaved trees and the more recently introduced conifers, but an acceptable compromise now appears to have been reached.

Other significant changes over the last 150 years have been more gradual and therefore less perceptible. What was once to all appearances an untouched wilderness has now been fragmented by railways and motor roads. There has been a vast increase in residential development, and around the margins of the Forest have been established an airfield and various industrial complexes. There are now very few areas of the Forest which remain unaffected by the sight or sound of modern technology, and it is this development that represents the present danger. Extreme care must be exercised if the beauty, character and uniqueness of the New Forest is to continue to survive.

Two

Buried relics of the past

ANTHONY PASMORE

The importance of the New Forest to the archaeologist lies in the fragile traces of ancient agriculture, forestry and industrial processes which have survived in this uncultivated region long after their destruction in more developed areas. The Forest can boast none of the spectacular stone circles, Roman villas or major defensive earthworks which are popular tourist attractions elsewhere, but the lesser sites which it does possess are rare and therefore of particular interest. Wherever man has lived or worked in the Forest he has left his mark in the form of earthworks – boundary banks and ditches, cattle pounds, coppice enclosures, burial mounds and industrial waste. There is little natural stone here, and local building materials were usually derived directly from the soil or what grew upon it. Earth being the most plentiful and durable of these resources has survived most widely.

The Bronze Age round barrows (of which there are well over one hundred in the Forest) are the best known of these earthworks. Large rounded mounds, sometimes forming a skyline feature as at Black Down, Map 8, or the Butt, Fritham, Map 3 are scattered throughout the district with the largest concentrations around Beaulieu. Many have been badly damaged by vandalism and uncontrolled excavation, but the rewards of this plundering have been fitting. Unlike the rich burials of surrounding counties, the Forest's barrows contained no more than patches of charcoal or an occasional decayed clay urn.

The defensive enclosures of the Forest are confined to one or two small hilltop forts, tentatively ascribed to the Iron Age. Of these, only Castle Hill at Burley, Map 9, and Castle Piece, Roe Inclosure, Map 5, are open to the public, although there are others on private land. Linear earthworks which appear to be of a defensive character may be seen to the

west of Hatchet Pond, Map 16, and at Red Hill, Map 11, but evidence as to the origin and purpose of these banks is lacking.

The Roman occupation has left little surviving trace within the Forest's boundaries. An important native pottery industry flourished here in the third and fourth centuries, and examples of its products may be seen in local museums. One reputed Roman road has been traced from Nursling to Stoney Cross, but the best preserved sections of this at Cadnam were destroyed by the construction of the M27 in 1974. Another earthwork claimed by some authorities as a Roman road may be seen in Fawley and Hardley Inclosures, Map 13. It seems that the Romans, like many of their successors, avoided major development of the poor land and difficult country presented by the New Forest.

In historic times the evidence for dating some of the Forest's sites is more plentiful. For example, the sites of six royal hunting lodges of the thirteenth to fifteenth centuries have recently been discovered. The most accessible of these is at Bolderwood, Map 6, where the present keeper's cottage is within a few yards of the original site. Five of these lodges occupied commanding positions overlooking the surrounding country for miles around, although they all now lie in densely wooded areas. They were in most cases probably little more than overnight camping places with a simple timber building roofed with thatch or slate and surrounded by a ditch, but we know from documentary sources that one at least (yet to be discovered) was a more elaborate structure with a chapel, stables and other buildings.

While the king was engaged in hunting, his subjects were probably more interested in the less exciting activity of pig keeping. The small pounds – earth banked inclosures once surmounted by a hedge or rails – survive in the more remote parts of the Forest. Some may date from as early as the eleventh century and due to their very slight construction they are difficult to locate on the ground. There are examples at Pinnick Wood and to the west of the Bishop's Dyke. These pounds were probably related to the commoners' rights of pannage, and they provided a comfortable and secure home for the pigs to return to at night.

Farming on a larger scale, often by illegal enclosure from the Open Forest, is represented by abandoned field systems in many parts of the district. The most extensive is at Crockford, Map 16 (355995) where the boundary banks cover nearly one hundred acres. This system may be medieval in origin, but encroachments continued well into the nineteenth century and were generally on a smaller scale. Tiny paddocks were taken in by cottagers during periods of agricultural prosperity, and were then abandoned in a subsequent depression or were re-possessed by the Crown. Good examples of these "Forest edge encroachments" may be seen at Beaulieu Rails (367990) and Hill Top, Map 13 (401040).

The Crown also made enclosures in the Open Forest, and among the earliest of these were extensive parks for the deer, constructed in order to facilitate hunting. The Park Pale at Lyndhurst is the best authenticated of these and dates from at least the late twelfth century. Its massive banks with their internal ditch are well preserved at Matley, The Ridge, Map 7. Other smaller deer enclosures of uncertain date survive at Denny, Map 7 (Stag Park) and Holm Hill, Map 6, the former being close to the road through the wood.

Later Crown enclosures were made for timber production, at first in small irregular shaped blocks for coppice wood, and then in large tracts of over 300 acres. Most of the latter date from 1700 onwards, and many still carry fences on top of the old banks. Coppice enclosures are earlier (sixteenth and seventeenth centuries), and their remains can be seen in New Copse Inclosure and the Round Hill Camp Site, Map 11 (335020).

Apart from the pastoral activities of the Forest population, there were occasional related industrial processes which have left their mark. An abortive attempt at saltpetre production in Elizabethan times has left an abandoned factory site near Ashurst Lodge, and bricks were produced in many parts of the Forest. The old clay pits are clearly visible at Park Grounds where the remains of the kiln can be seen adjoining the main road. Charcoal burning by the old pit method died out here fifty years ago, but the slight charcoal circles up to 60 feet across survive for centuries, and can still be found with a little practice. There are many in the woods around Lyndhurst and Beaulieu.

1 *Pottery find, Sloden.* [RF]
2 *Black Down Barrow.* [RF]
3 *Castle Hill, Burley, from Picket – Burley road.* [RF]
4 *Roman Road, Fawley Inclosure.* [RF]

Three

The ecology of the Forest

COLIN TUBBS

Since the eighteenth century dramatic changes have occurred in the English countryside. Successive tides of reclamation from the wild, each lapping a higher shoreline than its predecessor, have left us today with little more than fragments of wilderness. Through a series of historical accidents the economic pressures for radical change were largely deflected from the New Forest so that it now embraces the most extensive tract of unsown, or semi-natural, vegetation in the lowlands of Britain – gently contoured mosaic of woodland, heathland and acid grassland with valley bogs and in places fertile alluvial "lawns" marking the drainage pattern. It is important to appreciate that this is not a "primeval" landscape. It has been shaped since prehistoric times by man and his animals. The heathlands and grasslands have arisen as a secondary condition to an early woodland cover, the clearance of the woodland commencing at least as early as the Middle Bronze Age and continuing into modern times, though checked after the eleventh century by the

Forest Law, which protected the woodland against exploitation if not from the depredations of deer and the commoners' animals. Indeed, the large numbers of deer maintained in the Royal Forest, together with the commoners' animals, limited the regeneration and expansion of the woodlands.

The age structure of the unenclosed woodlands today is closely related to the fluctuations which took place in the numbers of these herbivores over the past three centuries or more. The long centuries of grazing and browsing have also much modified the species composition of the woods, for example by eliminating palatable shrubs like hazel and by impoverishing the ground flora. The commoners' animals have aptly been described as the architects of the Forest's scenery.

It is thought that few of the remaining areas of heathland in lowland Britain are large enough to support indefinitely many of their characteristic plants and animals. The New Forest is thus ecologically important because it offers the best chance of conserving the most

1

2

1 *Beefsteak fungus*. [RF]
2 *Wild gladiolus*. [RF]
3 *Dartford warbler*. [NO]

3

complete spectrum of the heathland flora and fauna. The fauna includes such birds as the woodlark, stonechat, Dartford warbler and nightjar; reptiles like the sand lizard and smooth snake; and butterflies such as the attractive silver-studded blue and the grayling. All these species have declined in Britain and the most important contributory factor has been the loss of their habitats. All occur in the New Forest and for some it is now their main stronghold in this country.

The Forest's bogs comprise deposits of saturated peat, accumulated in hollows and valleys. Because they receive some of the products of leaching on the higher ground the bogs tend to be base-enriched in contrast to the acid environments of their catchments. The central watercourses are often marked by alder or willow carr and the flanking vegetation is generally dominated by tussocks of purple moor grass. The bogs are floristically the Forest's richest habitats and their flora includes many local and rare species, like the marsh gentian and bog orchid. They also support a rich invertebrate fauna, including such specialised and rare insects as the tiny damsel fly and the impressive large marsh grasshopper. In the spring they come alive with the calls of breeding lapwing, redshank, curlew, snipe and other marsh birds. For the naturalist they are among the Forest's gems. Scientifically they are some of the finest remaining examples of their kind in western Europe.

The unenclosed woodlands no longer have any strict parallel in Britain. Lowland woods in which man does not shorten the natural life-span of the trees by felling are now rare and, outside the Forest, survive only as small fragments. The Forest woods are the finest relics of relatively undisturbed deciduous forest in Britain and probably in the lowlands of western Europe. They are mainly of oak, beech and holly and their essential ecological characteristics are their varied age structure; the abundance of mature, senile and decaying trees; and a rich epiphytic lichen and moss flora and insect, bird and bat fauna. The large bird populations of the woods depend mainly on the rich invertebrate fauna, which in turn is associated mainly with the abundant old timber. Birds characteristic of the woods include many which are rather locally distributed elsewhere, such as the redstart and wood warbler. As to be expected, hole and crevice nesters including woodpeckers, the nuthatch, tree-creeper, stock dove and the tits (except, notably, the willow tit) are particularly numerous. The woodland edges and glades are the habitat of two New Forest "specialities" one an insect, the other a plant – the New Forest cicada and the wild gladiolus, neither of which occur elsewhere in Britain.

The Inclosures have their own special species, besides forming extensive refuges for the Forest's larger mammals – deer, badgers and foxes. Breeding birds include crossbills, goldcrests and firecrests, all of which are associated with conifers, whilst the old oak plantations possess a flora and fauna sometimes approaching that of the unenclosed woodlands in variety.

In addition to those already outlined, two further factors contribute to the variety and well-being of the Forest's wildlife. First, the area is largely free from the use of toxic chemicals in agriculture or forestry; and secondly, because it is not used for game-rearing it possesses large populations of predatory birds such as buzzards, kestrels, sparrowhawks, tawny owls and others, which despite legal protection are persecuted elsewhere because they are still regarded as vermin.

Diversity is the ecological keynote of the New Forest. It possesses great variety of soils, habitats, plants and animals. Moreover, it includes large and ecologically viable areas of habitats which elsewhere in lowland Britain have been largely lost to agricultural reclamation, afforestation and development. It is a fair claim that today the New Forest is a unique reservoir of wildlife.

1

1 *Female Emperor moth displaying under-wing.* [HA]
2 *Adder.* [RF]
3 *Smooth snake.* [RF]
4 *Stag-headed oak tree near Queen's Bower.* [HA]
5 *Grass snake swallowing a mouse.* [RF]
6 *Heath Spotted orchid.* [TH]
7 *A Coral fungus.* [RF]

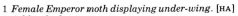

Four

Ships and Timber

New Forest timber and the Navy

David J Stagg

It is a mistake to regard a medieval forest as being nothing more than a royal game preserve, a place where the King could find amusement and relaxation. In practice the forests were of great economic significance, the deer being a necessary source of meat and their skins being used for a multitude of purposes from clothing to writing materials.

At the same time the Forest provided a source of building material for the royal houses. In 1250 the Keeper of the New Forest was ordered to prepare 20 000 shingles for roofing the King's Lodge at Clarendon and two years later a further 30 000 shingles were ordered for the same purpose. Revenue was obtained from the Forest in the form of fines imposed upon offenders against the Forest Laws, from the charging of rents in return for grazing privileges and also from the renting of Crown lands to private tenants.

Much wood and timber from the Forest was used for the construction of fortifications. As early as 1379 it is recorded that New Forest timber was supplied for Southampton defences and in later times timber was sent to Guernsey, the Isle of Wight, and Portsmouth, Southsea and Hurst Castles for use in fortifications. In the New Forest the first mentioned felling of timber for the Navy appears to be in 1611 when 1 800 oaks were supplied but supplies to the Navy remained intermittent until the latter half of the seventeenth century which saw the re-establishment of Portsmouth as one of the more important dockyards, also a rapid increase in the tonnage of the Navy.

1 *Buckler's Hard in 1805.*
H.M.S. Swiftsure *and H.M.S.* Euryalus *under construction, from a model at Beaulieu Maritime Museum.* [RF]

1

From about 1670 onwards a regular, if very small, supply of Navy timber was taken from the New Forest and on average this was 300 oak and 100 beech each year. It is impossible to know how many trees were actually felled as it would appear that a great quantity of timber was stolen. It is recorded in 1671 that much of the timber for a frigate then framing in the Forest has been embezzled by the carpenters and workmen. In the dockyard the small chips were by custom the carpenters' perquisites but under this pretence much good timber was stolen.

In 1670 some 300 acres had been planted as nurseries for timber and for this purpose the woodward was instructed to gather 1 000 bushels of acorns and 1 000 bushels of beech mast, also hawthorn berries and sloes. The hawthorn and sloes, also known as white-thorn and blackthorn, were planted to provide ground cover for the protection of the growing trees. At this time the Forest's stock of red deer had just been replenished by the gift of 60 stags from the King of France and both in planting and in felling the well-being of the deer was a first consideration. Objections were made to the use of Holm Hill as a nursery for timber, it being "a place very much delightful for the feeding and harbouring of His Majesty's deer" and when timber was cut it was not to be done "injurious to the beauty of the park or the shelter of the deer".

A survey of the timber made in 1707 reported that there were only 12 476 oaks suitable for the Navy. This has frequently been taken to mean a general depletion of the woodlands but in fact it was an indication of a serious failure in their administration as regards the production of Navy timber. Further surveys made in 1764 and 1782 show a steadily improving situation but the needs of the Navy were increasing at an even faster rate. A further 1 000 acres of oak had been planted in 1700, and a little more towards the end of the eighteenth century but finally, in 1808, an extensive programme was begun and 12 000 acres of oak were planted during the next sixty years. Of course it was too late.

New Forest oak today

David J Stagg

The oaks planted as a result of the New Forest Inclosure Act of 1808 were destined never to sail the seas, with one curious exception. Some New Forest oak timber was used in the 1939–45 war to build wooden mine sweepers. These ships were safe from an otherwise deadly weapon – the German magnetic mine. Wooden ships were replaced by ironclads and 1862 was the last year in which a considerable quantity of Navy timber was supplied from the New Forest. Oak is, however, regularly used on a large scale for Scottish fishing vessels. Today there remain some 5 000 acres of mature, even-aged oak plantations within the Statutory Inclosures. Eventually these will be replaced by woodland of mixed ages but it is the intention that they should be retained as long as possible as a most interesting example of eighteenth-nineteenth century silviculture and a unique memorial to the age of wooden ships.

The wooden walls of England

David Cobb

In the eyes of the British Shipwright, English Oak (*Quercus robur*) was the best ship timber in the world and at the time of the Tudors the country was well-supplied with oak on a scale to meet all foreseeable needs. Yet over the next two centuries massive depletions took place, the greatest devourer being the iron industry which needed charcoal for smelting; ships of war and merchant ships also consumed large quantities; domestic buildings, casks for beer and wine competed for the available supplies. The land was scoured for its trees without regard to their replacement.

The oak shortage struck the Navy towards

the end of the seventeenth century, when the hasty use of unseasoned wood to meet demands for new ships wasted England's available ship timber with nothing more to show for it than some rotting hulks.

Urgent action was overdue, as an oak must grow for a hundred years before it can be used in a ship. Parliament's eyes fell upon the Royal Forests: the Dean, the New Forest and Alice Holt. In 1698 a New Forest Act provided for 2 000 acres of trees to be planted and 200 acres a year for twenty years. By 1725, however, these policies has fallen into complete neglect and during 57 years in the eighteenth century the total output of all the Royal Forests amounted to no more than four years' naval supply, the balance being made up from provident private estates and increasingly from abroad.

Between 1745 and 1818 some fifty vessels were built by contract at Buckler's Hard, Beaulieu, including the famous warships *Agamemnon (64 guns)*, *Swiftsure (74 guns)* and *Euryalus (36 guns)*. From such a small yard over a short period this is a fine record; the Royal dockyards took longer to build a ship and their costs of construction were greater.

The *Agamemnon*, which was the smallest type of ship fit to fight in line of battle, required 2 000 mature oak trees in its construction in 1781, apart from other timber such as elm and beech for planking.

Ship-building timber was classified into mast, plank and compass. The latter came from the curved branches whose shape adapted easily to the frames or ribs of the hull. New Forest oak was more productive of compass timber than of plank, which had to be in long straight runs.

Timber accounted for half the cost of construction of a wooden ship, which in the Napoleonic period was reckoned to be about £1 000 per gun. Thus the *Agamemnon* would have cost some £65 000 without ordnance. Durability had a marked effect on overall costs: Nelson's Victory cost only £63 174 when she was launched in 1765, by the time she fought at Trafalgar repairs had swelled this to £251 981 and by 1815 she had cost the country some £371 922. Even more astronomical sums would no doubt have been expended on the Queen Charlotte had not the Navy sensibly cut its losses when she rotted away almost completely within two years of her launch, without ever putting to sea. Yet the *Royal*

William, built in 1719, lasted for nearly a century without expensive repairs.

Properly seasoned, oak, as Evelyn wrote, is "tough, bending well, strong and not too heavy, nor easily admitting water". In 1805 some one and a half million oak trees were at sea in the shape of the British Navy. Today the oceans carry steel and fibreglass; the hearts of oak are no more.

1

2

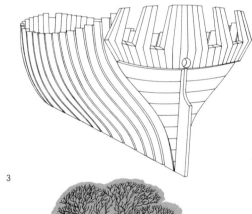

3

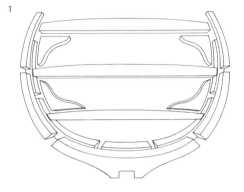

24

4

5

1 *A detail of the midship section of a wooden ship.*
2 *An indication of the volume of framing timber required for a wooden ship (nineteenth century) before the planking is in place.*
3 *Some typical shapes of shipwright timber provided by the oak.*
4 *Blackwood's frigate* Euryalus *(launched at Buckler's Hard in 1803) which brought about the interception of the Combined Fleet by Nelson at Trafalgar.* [DAVID COBB]
5 *Frontispiece of* New Forest *by Percival Lewis, 1811. Engraving by C. Sheringham.* [RF]

Five

Place names and personalities

ARTHUR T LLOYD

To an historian the names on a map summon up the past and supply vital clues to events which might otherwise be lost. They are living sign-posts, but caution is needed, as frequently the obvious meaning is not the correct one.

The oldest place names in this area are those of the waterways that bound the Forest, namely the Avon (Celtic word for "river") and Solent (origin uncertain). Flowing through the Forest is the Lymington river; the prefix means "elm".

Iron Age hill forts were usually called in Saxon times "bury". South west Hampshire has several, such as Burley, Tatchbury and Exbury. The name "Rings" at Buckland also indicates such a fort. But in the case of Holbury the suffix may refer to a Roman building, and the prefix show its ruined state (in holes). "Drakenhorde" in Rockbourne probably points to the discovery of a Roman treasure; it is close to the fine villa found in 1942. Similarly, Hordle, south of the Forest, means "treasure hill".

One reference in Domesday shows that as late as William I's reign people remembered the Celtic name "Andret" for this stretch of woodland along the south east coast. On the death in 1100 of William Rufus a chronicler wrote that the old name for the New Forest was "Ytene". Philologists have known for eighty years that this means "(land) of the Jutes", proving Bede's assertion about 730 that the Jutes had settled in southern Hampshire as well as the Isle of Wight and Kent.

The Forest has interesting links with the Saxon Royal House, for the Chronicler stated that Cerdic landed in 495 at "Cerdicesora", which might be Ower, Calshot. Cerdic's battle in 508 against the Britons led by Natanleod may have taken place at Nateley; if so, the name is derived from that of the chief. These are surmises, but with Charford we have a name that is definitely derived from Cerdic's battle in 519 at "Cerdicesford".

Eling is the next oldest name of Saxon origin in this area, meaning "Edla's followers". Ellingham, far to the west, means "homestead of Eling men". Keeping, in the Beaulieu area, may be a Jutish type of -ing name. Canterton near Brook, "farm of men from Kent", shows a link with the earlier Jutish settlements there.

South-west Hampshire may have been the last English area to retain its Germanic heathenism. Here two heathen Jutish princes fled in 680 from the Island. Nearby, in the bounds of Millbrook, Thunor was worshipped – the god who gave his name to Thursday. On the Forest's western bounds are Godshill and Devilsden the latter being named in 1300.

Place names prove the area was well-wooded in early times. Six incorporate the word "wood", besides another five on the Forest edge like Arne- ("Eagle"), Ring- ("edge") and Wootton ("farm in the wood"). Lyndhurst ("lime tree wooded hill"), Brockenhurst (possibly "badger hill wood") and Bramshaw ("bramble copse") tell the same story. So do the 36 examples in the Forest and 25 nearby of the ending -ley, meaning "wood" or "clearing". Oakley, Bartley ("birch") and Ashley specify the tree species; others give each owner's name, as Sopley and Woodfidley: the latter's owner was probably a lady, Wulfgyth. Apple and Alder also appear as prefixes, as does Maple in the lost Domesday name "Mapleham".

The Danes, of course, made little impact. Only "Colgrimesmore" on the Beaulieu bounds in John's reign is definitely Danish, whereas the name Dane Stream arising near Wootton is derived from the Saxon "denu" (valley). A few Norman names survive, especially in the area of Beaulieu, itself of course French, from the Latin "Bellus locus regis", where kings had owned a hunting lodge before the Abbey was founded. On Abbey lands are Beufre and Bergerie (beef and sheep farms). The word "Purlieu" is used, associated with Dibden and Ogden, and close to the Forest edge are Hinton Admiral, and the Albamarlia family, and Tiptoe, the name a family brought with them from their Norman village.

Of course, the name New Forest derives from William I's afforestation. Domesday named 45 manors reduced to little value once the King's

1 *Avon River viewed from Castle Hill.* [DS]
2 *Bolton's Bench, Lyndhurst at sunset.* [RF]
3 *Boldre Church, associated with Gilpin.* [RF]

hunting took precedence. Of those identified only recently, the most important historically is "Thorougham", wrongly linked with Fritham (homestead in woodland) since the eighteenth century. It is definitely the area now Park Farm, on the Beaulieu Estate. Its significance comes from it being the site identified earlier than any other with the death of Rufus.

When William I created the Forest his officials and local people had to know its bounds. Named tumuli, for example Lugden's Barrow and Knave's Ash on West boundary, were used; more interesting is "Rodedic" on the bounds, for this was a meeting place for the local Hundred. Within the Forest is Bishop's Dyke, which is said to demarcate an area round which the Bishop of Winchester crawled in one day to secure land for his church. Queen's Bower must be the medieval hunting lodge called "Queneboure" (named after Eleanor, wife of Edward I).

At the end of the Middle Ages, both the widow of Warwick the Kingmaker and Perkin Warbeck claimed sanctuary at Beaulieu, but soon all such monastic property fell into lay hands. The Forest saw many armed horsemen again in the Civil War, but it must be remembered that Marryat's children's story is all fiction.

It was Charles II who enclosed New Park near Brockenhurst, and it was his brother's judge (Jeffreys) who dealt so harshly with Dame Alice Lisle of Moyles Court, after Monmouth failed to reach Lymington and escape by boat.

Bolton's Bench commemorates a member of that Ducal family which held the office of Master Keeper of Burley Bailiwick throughout the eighteenth century.

In Boldre churchyard lies asleep the Reverend William Gilpin, lover of the Forest scene; the historian John Wise is buried in the new cemetery at Lyndhurst, the grave of Sir Arthur Conan Doyle is at Minstead, Brusher Mills the snake catcher is buried in Brockenhurst churchyard, and in the family vault at Lyndhurst parish church lies Alice Hargreaves, who as a little girl was given immortality as Lewis Carroll's Alice.

Where the Forest begins to slope towards the sea, Peterson's Sway Tower built in 1884 stands as a curious memorial to one man's faith in reinforced concrete as a material for building.

Six

William Rufus

The strange death of William Rufus

John Chapman

"On the morrow of Lammas, King William was killed with an arrow while hunting by one of his men". Thus ended, according to the Anglo-Saxon Chronicle, on 2 August 1100 in its thirteenth year, the reign of William II of England, third son of William the Conqueror, done to death in his father's New Forest, which had already claimed two of his kinsmen.

Nothing else is known for certain about the King's death and it is partly because of the mystery surrounding it that the tragedy today still casts a lurid glow out of England's savage past like those fires of hell to which so many of the King's subjects thought his soul had descended.

Some twenty years later two men who had been living at the time wrote more circumstantial accounts and although they differ in detail both agree that an arrow loosed by one Walter Tirel at a stag by mischance entered the body of his sovereign. Tirel apparently fled immediately to France and the fact that no attempt seems to have been made to investigate the matter in any way supports the common assumption of the time that the King's death was an accident.

Rufus was a cynical, greedy and determined ruler, small, thickset, ill-shaped, his face redder than his hair, his eyes of two different colours, and his oppression of the Church and dissolute ways had made him many enemies amongst his subjects. Small wonder then that stories of dreadful portents began to circulate which with hindsight seemed to suggest that he was destined for calamity in retribution for his sins.

He is said to have dreamed the night before he died of a gout of blood spurting up from his breast to obscure the sun. The Earl of Cornwall, hunting in a distant wood, met a black goat with the body of a naked man wounded on its back and crying "I bear to judgment your King, or rather your tyrant, William Rufus. For I am a malevolent spirit and the avenger of his wickedness which raged against the Church of Christ and so I have procured his death".

Some later anthropologists have gone further and suggested that the King went voluntarily to his death as a scapegoat for the sins of his people, the sacrificial victim of an ancient fertility cult surviving in Europe under the veneer of Christianity, but this can be no more than supposition.

The possibility that the Red King was murdered is a much more tenable theory and is consistent with the evidence. His younger brother, Henry, was a member of the fatal hunting party and as soon as he learned of his brother's death he left for Winchester where he demanded the keys to the King's treasury as the lawful heir. He then rode to London and procured his own coronation as Henry I on 5 August, only three days later. This was a remarkable feat by any standards and would have been difficult enough if planned in advance. Perhaps it was. Certainly the timing was favourable: the rightful heir, Robert, Duke of Normandy, was conveniently out of the country on a Crusade.

Tirel made good his escape and no action was ever taken against him; indeed he kept possession of lands he held in England and his brothers-in-law, the Clares, who were also members of the hunting party, prospered under the new King. Possibly there were compelling reasons for leaving him alone. He is said in later years to have asserted that he was not with Rufus when he was slain but if he agreed to act the fugitive to protect someone else there is no record of any reward given to him save immunity from reprisals.

Unfortunately we shall never know. If there were a conspiracy to kill the King, it was most effectively concealed, as well it might be since the prize was the crown of England itself. And perhaps something more: a local historian, Marjorie Triggs, has pieced together from the records an intriguing theory about which she writes here for the first time.

Yet one more mystery remains to discuss: the exact place of Rufus's death. Much research on this subject has been done by Arthur Lloyd, who is now convinced that the generally accepted location in Canterton Glen is in fact the wrong one and that the King died near the present farm buildings at Park Farm on the Beaulieu Estate.

The earliest writer to mention the place

where the death occurred is Leland, who stated, some 440 years after the event, that it was at Thorougham. That place name became lost but the chief oral tradition indicated a tree in Canterton Glen and it was there that John, Lord Delaware, erected a stone on the site in 1745. The Reverend William Gilpin of Boldre, writing in 1790, suggested that Thorougham might have been what is now called Fritham, which is near Canterton.

Lloyd points out that Park Farm was originally called Thorougham and translates from the latin of the Annals of Waverley Abbey: "In the year 1204 King John once built a Cistercian Abbey which he named Bellus Locus near the spot where William Rufus the King was killed". Park Farm is only three and a half miles from Beaulieu whereas Canterton is about ten miles from the Abbey.

Again, Leland mentions a chapel at his Thorougham, of which there is no trace at Canterton whilst there are references to a

1 *The original Rufus Stone from Drivers Map, 1789.*
2 *Death of William for Barnard's* History of England.

chapel at Park Farm. The earliest known Royal hunting lodge in the Forest was at Beaulieu.

Arthur Lloyd's arguments, which he set out in full in Hampshire Magazine for September 1962, are persuasive but prompt one final doubt: if Leland's reference to Thorougham was mistaken, then the main link with Park Farm is broken. Again we shall probably never know.

"Did Rufus die for love of a lady?"

Marjorie Triggs

One version of the death of King William II tells us that, killed by an arrow, his body lay forlorn in the New Forest, forsaken by his hunting companions, who had fled in confusion, except for William de Breteuile who rode to Winchester to claim the throne for Robert, Duke of Normandy. The shot, through the heart, was a bulls-eye, the hallmark of the professional marksman. Was this then no mischance, but contrived accident . . . treason?

Rufus had no legal heir but a reciprocal treaty between him and his elder brother made Robert his heir.

Yet after the hasty interment of Rufus's body the next day Henry, the youngest of William the Conqueror's sons, claimed the Throne. Robert at this crucial time was far away Crusading and in spite of vigorous protest by William de Breteuile on his behalf, Henry became King-elect, being crowned on 5 August.

Although already the father of several children by various mistresses Henry was also without legal heir and his counsellors urged him to marry. His choice was Eadgyth, daughter of Malcolm Canmore, King of Scotland and of his Queen Margaret, great granddaughter of Edmund Ironside, an early king of the English.

An intriguing story tells how, some years before, Rufus was so impressed by reports of the beauty and charms of youthful Eadgyth then staying with her aunt, the Abbess Christina, at Romsey, that he went to see her. Neither his dissolute reputation nor his appearance, described as repulsive, were likely to commend him to the Abbess or her niece. Fearful of his intentions Christina hastily dressed her ward in nun's habit and veil, sending her into the garden with other nuns. Greeting Rufus, she invited him into the garden to see her roses. Here he saw Eadgyth garbed as a nun, seemingly a novitiate, whereupon he left.

The fair Eadgyth came into the care of her aunt again at the death of her parents; perhaps she was living as a nun at Romsey when Henry became King. Wherever she was Henry put the case of their marriage before the newly returned and reinstated Archbishop Anselm. She was willing and eager to marry Henry; his plea spoke of his long-standing love for her, so this was no new or sudden desire.

Anselm convened an Assembly of dignitaries after whose deliberations he declared Eadgyth no nun and therefore free to marry Henry. On 11 November 1100 Eadgyth (or Edith) became his Queen Matilda, amidst public acclaim, for her Royal Saxon ancestry assured Henry's acceptance by the English as their king, firmly establishing his sovereignty.

While Rufus lived what hope did Henry have of achieving this marriage? For it has been said that when the question of Matilda leaving the Abbey had been raised, Rufus told Anselm that he wished her to remain there. If that was so Henry could hardly overcome his opposition, for Rufus was omnipotent.

Was this long-standing love for Matilda the deciding factor in Henry's unsurping the Throne, so that he could gain the power to release her from the cloistered life? Did then Rufus die for Henry's love of a lady, the desirable Matilda?

But how can we know what really happened, who can we truly believe when one of the early chroniclers has said how difficult it was to tell the exact truth "especially when Kings are concerned"? And . . . a certain Queen?

Seven

Smugglers and their ways

K MERLE CHACKSFIELD

"I have myself seen a procession of twenty or thirty waggons loaded with kegs of spirits; an armed man sitting at the front and tail of each; and surrounded by a troop of two or three hundred horsemen, every one carrying on his enormous saddle from two to four tubs of spirits; winding deliberately and with the most picturesque and imposing effect along the skirts of Hengistbury Head on their way towards the wild country north-west of Christchurch".

So wrote Richard Warner in his "Literary Recollections" published in 1830, and there is no doubt that during the eighteenth and nineteenth centuries such a scene might have been common on almost any part of the coast where the New Forest comes down to the sea and where the beaches and chines, or small ravines, running seawards, provided conditions ideal for smuggling.

This was a time when severe taxation, combined with the general poverty of the working people, led to smuggling on a very large scale. The operation consisted essentially of buying a shipload of dutiable goods across the Channel, shipping them to a lonely English beach, preferably by night, to be hidden away locally if necessary and eventually distributed into the country.

"Free trading", as it was called, became big business, and played an important part in the economic life of the people. Capital was invested, perhaps by the squire and local traders, doctors, farmers and even the parson, and at the other end of the scale it provided an extra source of income for farm labourers, fishermen and small tradesmen in those poverty-stricken times when a labourer's wage was seven shillings a week.

Tea, tobacco, brandy, silks, laces, pearls, spices and wines, even aristocrats escaping the French Revolution and gold and spies during the Napoleonic wars, all passed through the smugglers' hands.

Against this widespread activity was pitted on land the small forces of law in the shape of a Riding Officer of Customs and Excise with a handful of men, who could call upon the assistance of the Dragoons if there were any in the locality. The area patrolled by one such Officer extended from Poole to Hurst Castle. The Revenue Cutters did what they could to intercept the cargoes at sea, but as a naval commander reported in 1815, to order a

1 *Naked Man, Wilverley.* [KMC]

2 *Cat and Fiddle Inn.* [KMC]

Revenue Cutter to pursue a smuggling lugger was "like sending a cow after a hare".

The New Forest offered excellent cover for smuggling and its leafy ways and secret places were well known to the "free traders". In the Queen's Head, a seventeenth century inn at Burley, the smugglers would make their plans for handling cargoes expected at Chewton Bunny, a miniature gorge where a stream runs down from the Forest to the sea at Highcliffe. This was a most convenient landing place for goods destined for Burley, Ringwood, Fordingbridge and Salisbury. The contraband was brought up in waggons or on horseback along the track from the head of the Bunny over Chewton Common to the Cat and Fiddle Inn at Hinton, where the men would unload some of the tubs.

Smuggling was an activity usually carried on by men, but there were some women who delighted in taking part in the excitement and profit of the illicit trade. One such was Lovey Warne, a high-spirited girl who, with her brothers, Peter and John, occupied a cottage by the smugglers' path at Knave's Ash, between Crow and Burley. Her chief task was to warn the free-traders during the daytime of the presence of the Riding Officer. Dressed in a cloak of the brightest scarlet, she would stand whenever danger threatened at the top of Vereley Hill, close to Picket Post, from where she was clearly visible to the smugglers at almost every approach to Burley.

John King of Burley was a man who remembered smuggling days. He was "a big man like a gnarled oak, hard as iron", and he had many times taken "a couple of forest ponies with sacks on their backs and had gone down to the sea". He said that the smugglers' route was "across Crane's Moor, up the smugglers' path, through Vereley and Ridley up to Smugglers' Road there and on to Fritham".

It would seem that John King, even as an old man, was still active with "the Gentlemen" and he would bring kegs of brandy all the way from Barton Cliffs to a hiding place cleverly concealed under the hearth. The smugglers' would say:

"Keystone under the hearth" and

"Keystone under the horse's belly",

meaning that the contraband was hidden either under flagstones by the fire or under the stable floor.

It is probable that there was a smugglers' walk over Poor Man's Common to Picket Post

1 *Smuggler's spout lantern.* [KMC]

and it is suggested that there is still a bricked-up cellar somewhere beneath the bracken where contraband was hidden.

A difficult area to cover when being pursued by the preventive men was the open heathland at Thorney Hill. During one hot chase, the horses and a waggon-load of goods were driven straight into the great barn at Chubb's or possibly Atkin's Farm. The farmer there, when questioned by the preventive men as to the whereabouts of the free-traders, pretended that he had been bowled over by the waggon and that his leg was broken. He said that if they rode hard they might catch up with them further on in the village of Burley.

Cargoes landed at Lymington, Milford and Milton were often taken up the Boldre River into the Forest, and further east the Beaulieu River formed another route from the coast.

Punishment for convicted smugglers was harsh and included transportation and even hanging. By the roadside at Mark Way, near Wilverley Post on the A35, stands on the lonely heath, surrounded by a protective fence, the insignificant remains of what was once a great tree known as the Naked Man. From its stout boughs many malefactors, highwaymen as well as smugglers, paid the penalty of their wrongdoings at the end of the hangman's rope.

When you see ponies cropping the green sward of the Forest, or stumble upon a sunken track half hidden in the young bracken; or perhaps when you sail the tidal waters of the Beaulieu River along Fiddler's Reach to Buckler's Hard, you may remember the "Gentlemen of the Night", who used these ways over two hundred years ago and risked transportation or hanging for two shillings and sixpence a keg, or five shillings for a night's smuggling.

Eight

The Commoner

HUGH C PASMORE

A New Forest commoner is a person who, by virtue of occupying land to which attaches a Right of Common, as registered in 1858, is entitled to certain privileges, all of which originate from the distant past.

The farming commoner is much influenced by his use of these rights for though he may himself occupy only a few acres, his ability to take advantage of the forest enables him to farm on a comparatively large scale. On the other hand there are many modern commoners who do not actually farm but have a full time job in the district, for even a garden plot to which attaches the appropriate right entitles the occupier to "farm" the forest.

There are five Rights of Common in the Forest and these are described below:

COMMON OF PASTURE is the most valuable right and enables the commoner to depasture animals on some 45 000 acres of open forest. This right of grazing is believed to date from the days of William the Conqueror when the New Forest was a hunting preserve and local husbandmen were prohibited from fencing any of their land lest it interfere with the Monarch's sport. It was recognised that this imposed on the farmer a very great hardship and he was therefore permitted to allow his beasts to wander over the forest for five summer months (excluding four weeks in June/July – Fence month (20 June to 20 July – when the does normally dropped their fawns). During the winter months (Winter Heyning – 22 November to 4 May) when keep was scarce the right was withdrawn so that the deer would not go short.

Over the years extensive changes have taken place and in 1851 an Act of Parliament decreed that all deer should be destroyed or removed from the forest in return for the commoners' agreement that 10 000 acres of open land should be fenced and used for timber production. Thus today commonable animals have a legal right to remain on the forest for the whole of the year, though in fact deer have re-established themselves throughout the forest.

It has become a fairly constant pattern that about 5 000 commonable animals run on the forest and in recent times the number of ponies has exceeded the cattle by three to two. Donkeys will be found mainly in the north and west on light or sandy soils but seldom number more than fifty.

The number of commoners actually using

1 *Cattle and ponies grazing on Broomy Plain.* [RF]

1

1

their rights of turning animals on to the forest is in the region of 350 but this is only a fraction of those entitled to do so. In the office of the Clerk to the Verderers are maps prepared by the Forestry Commission showing all the land to which common rights attach and these may be inspected on payment of a nominal fee. Lands bearing rights stretch well outside the forest boundary, even as far away as Bournemouth and Cranborne.

The right to run cattle on the forest is of inestimable value to farmers whose land adjoins the forest, for during wet weather instead of his land being "poached" or cut up by his herd the animals are fed and remain outside, only coming in for milking or veterinary attention. Ponies on the other hand remain permanently on the forest and may well "haunt" (the foresters' name for the district a pony inhabits) an area many miles from its owner's farm, where fortunately for the owner it usually remains within a radius of two or three miles throughout its life.

Though commonable animals (ponies, cattle, pigs and a few sheep) run on the forest as of legal right, they are subject to Byelaws imposed by the Court of Verderers under statutory powers and the owner pays to the Court a grazing fee in respect of each one. Currently

(1986) this amounts to £10 per head per annum and is collected by the Agisters for the Court to use to defray the cost of supervising and controlling the animals.

No commonable animal may graze upon the forest unless it is branded with its owner's mark and the Verderers maintain a complete register of these identification brands. Traditionally, ponies are branded on the left or near side in one of three places: on the back where the saddle normally sits, on the shoulder or on the hip. Cattle on the other hand are branded on the right or off side flank. Pony branding is done by clipping the hair as short as possible and then "touching" the hide with a red hot branding iron. It is now illegal to use this method for cattle and they are marked by a chemical application that turns the hair permanently white. Many forest farmers use brand designs which have been handed down through generations of their families.

In addition to the forest Right of Pasture there are others less widely used today, though in the past they also were much prized by the commoner.

COMMON OF MAST is the right to turn pigs on to the forest during what is known as the

1 *Pigs at pannage in Rhinefield.* [RF]
2 *Assignment fuelwood.* [HA]
3 *Mare and foal.* [RF]
4 *Sample of commoners' brands for ponies, Green Dragon Brook.* [HI]

Pannage Season when acorns and beech-mast have fallen and provide excellent feed for pigs, though when green are poisonous to cattle and ponies when taken to excess. Until the New Forest Act of 1964 Pannage dates were fixed from 25 September to 22 November but in those seasons when the acorn fall was late, pigs in search of food invaded local gardens, hence the Act provided for the Forestry Commission after consultation with the Verderers to fix any suitable term of not less than sixty days. The commoner pays a small fee per animal to the Verderers. On the 3 500 acres of private commons which march with the true forest, local commoners are not subject to the Pannage dates and there pigs roam throughout the year.

COMMON OF TURBARY entitled the commoner to cut turf for burning in his dwelling, the rule being that for every turf cut the two adjoining ones must be left, thereby avoiding stripping the area completely. Only one or two commoners avail themselves of this right today.

COMMON OF FUELWOOD, sometimes referred to as Estovers or Assignment Wood. The Forestry Commission allocates one or more cords of burning wood to certain tenements to which this registered right attaches and as in the case of Turbary the wood has to be burnt in the house. Over the years these rights have diminished in number and today only some eighty commoners enjoy allocations. The Forestry Commission cuts and stacks the wood, usually reasonably close to the commoner's holding, and assigns the correct cordage to the rightholder who has to collect it.

COMMON OF MARL. This is a right to take Marl from the twenty-three forest pits for spreading on the commoner's land as a form of manuring. Modern agricultural methods have now rendered this right more or less obsolete.

In 1909 the New Forest commoners formed an Association known as the New Forest Commoners' Defence Association and today with over 500 members the Association still fulfills its original function of safeguarding the members' rights, whilst at the same time forming a valuable link with the Forestry Commission and the Court of Verderers whereby many difficult forest problems are solved.

35

Nine

The Verderers

MALDWIN DRUMMOND

The title Verderer comes from the Norman word "vert" meaning green and referring to woodland. William the Conqueror set aside vast areas for hunting, creating "forest" protected by new laws and officials. In these, the "vert" and the "venison" (the flesh of beasts of the Forest: red, fallow and roe deer and wild boar) were for the benefit of the King.

The Verderers were part of the judicial and administrative hierarchy of the Forest. This system was modified in 1238, when the Forests of England were divided into two provinces, one north and the other south of the River Trent. A Chief Justice was appointed for each province and he travelled around on circuit, hence the name of his Court, that of the Chief Justice in Eyre (errer – old French for journey). This was the senior Forest Court, being dependent on the lesser court of "Attachment" and on "Inquisitions" for its clients.

The duty of the court of "Attachment", on which Verderers sat, was to investigate and record "attachments" made by officials of the Forest. It could only deal with minor vert offences and had a limit of 4d on the fines it could impose. In addition, the Court administered such things as wood rights and swore in Forest officials.

More serious offences, such as venison, were "attached" to the Court of the Chief Justice in Eyre.

"Inquisitions" investigated the death of one of the King's deer in much the same way as a coroner's court today, though the carcase was sent to "the spittal house or given to the sick and poor", while the head went to the freemen of the nearest town and the arrow was presented to a Verderer as evidence; the poor accused, if found, languished in jail to await the coming of the Court of the Chief Justice in Eyre.

"Assarts" or the illegal cultivation of land, "purpresture" or illegally erecting structures or digging fish ponds, were reported to the court by the "Regarders", an independent team of watchdogs who visited every three years. They also had charge of the "lawing of dogs". This was the multilation of three toes of the fore feet to prevent their harming the deer, if they were of the size to do so. The "Stirrup of Rufus" (actually a Tudor relic) in the Verderers' Hall was said to have been such a measure, for if the dog could pass through it he need not be so cruelly treated. The necessity though was usually overcome through payment of a fine or a bribe. It is said that the Regarders used to go through the towns blowing their horns to cause concealed and potentially deer-hungry dogs to bark and so reveal themselves.

The Assembly or Court of Swainmote, through which the Verderers superintended the pannage of pigs and the removal of cattle during the summer fence month and winter heyning (periods when the open waste of the Forest was reserved strictly for the King's deer), was sometimes allied to the Court of Attachment. Presentments could be made to this Court by the aggrieved. The distinction between the two "courts" became blurred and they exist as one today.

Then, as now, they were held in the Verderers' Hall at Lyndhurst. This was built within or beside the manor house of the Royal Manor of Lyndhurst in 1388. The old entrance used to be through the Tudor porch and was altered during the substantial changes to the Hall and the Queen's House in 1851. The panelling that lines the walls of the present court came from the upper rooms destroyed in the Victorian change. The Honourable Gerald Lascelles, however, built his offices above the Hall and restored the outside appearance of the old building to roughly what it was before 1851 and is again today.

Before the final demise of the supreme

"Forest" Court of the Chief Justice in Eyre in 1817, after long redundancy, attempts had been made to strengthen the Courts of Swainmote and Attachment in Acts of 1698 and 1800, but the real change did not take place until the passing of the New Forest Act 1877, or "Commoners' Charter" as it came to be called.

Under this Act, the number of Verderers was increased to seven, the Official Verderer being appointed by the Crown. They were to be elected by registered commoners and those who were parliamentary voters of any parish or township wholly or partly within the perambulation. To be elected, a candidate for a Verderer must own not less than seventy five acres to which common rights attached. This and the method of election, which was not secret, the voter having to declare his choice openly to the polling clerk, ensured that few contested elections were held in seventy years.

The Act also gave the Verderers administrative duties to control the grazing and health of animals depastured on the Forest and to make byelaws and to regulate the exercise of the rights of common. The re-organised Court of Swainmote was given the status of petty sessions and the sitting Swainmote Verderers, powers of a Justice of the Peace.

In 1947 the Baker committee produced a report which reflected the changing role of the Forest.

The 1949 Act reconstituted this court. A register of those entitled to vote was to be maintained by the Verderers and polling stations designated where a secret ballot could take place in order to choose the five elective Verderers. One Verderer each was nominated by the following four authorities: the Forestry Commission, Ministry of Agriculture, Hampshire County Council and Countryside Commission.

1 *The Verderers' Court, Queen's House, Lyndhurst.*
[RP]

1

This new Act strengthened the powers of the Verderers' Court to control the health of animals, grazing and rights of common. The Verderers' Agisters carry out this day-to-day work on behalf of the Court. The Verderers were also given power to grant the Forestry Commission new Inclosures for timber production and for the regeneration of the Ancient and Ornamental Woodland. Ability was also given on presentment by the Minister to fence the Cadnam–Ringwood trunk road (A31). This was to lead, through the medium of the 1964 and 1970 Acts, to the fencing of the A35 and the fencing and gridding of the New Forest itself, embracing at the same time the outlying commons.

The Verderers' duties had passed from mainly judicial to administrative, encouraging and implementing advances in animal health, such as making the Forest the first unenclosed tuberculin tested (TT) area and the encouragement of conservation measures as embodied in the study "Conservation of the New Forest".

In 1877 the Court's time was taken up for the most part by the demands of the commoners and their animals. Today, although this is still a principal concern, the Court is increasingly involved in ensuring that the traditional life, beauty and unique natural history of the Forest is not spoilt by and for the hundreds of thousands that come to enjoy it, whether for the day or to camp and caravan.

The Verderers sit in "open" Court every two months on a Monday at 10.00 am. Any member of the public can make a "presentment", an ancient custom carried on from the Court of Swainmote. The senior Agister standing in the Court's old wooden dock and raising his right hand, invites this participation with the ancient message:

"Oyez, oyez, oyez!
All manner of persons who have any presentment or matter or thing to do at this Court of Swainmote, let him come forward and he shall be heard!
God Save The Queen!"

The relationship between the Forestry Commission and the Verderers has not always been happy because of the divergent interests of those who depasture cattle and those who are responsible for the production of timber. Perhaps it is because of the strong intervention of a third party, the public, that the Court and Commission now work in harmony for the benefit of all three. It is perhaps the happiest development from the Laws of William.

Ten

The Agisters

HUGH C PASMORE

It will be evident that with more than 5 000 commonable animals roaming over a hundred square miles of open forest, some form of supervision and control is essential. This control is provided by the Court of Verderers, whose constitution and powers have been described earlier. The Court appoints four men known as Agisters (derived from Norman "to receive payment"), whose duty it is to supervise all the commonable animals in that part of the forest which is allocated as their area. An important aspect of this work is the maintenance of good public relations with local residents and others affected by movements of the animals.

An obvious necessity for an Agister is that he should ride the forest to keep in touch with animals in the more remote parts, and he receives from the Verderers an allowance for the maintenance of a pony. Each man must be an accomplished horseman for much of his time is spent rounding up forest ponies which may well involve galloping across very rough country. He must also have an intimate knowledge of the very extensive area of woodland, moor and bog which constitutes his beat.

In addition, the Verderers have an arrange-ment with the Hampshire Police Authority whereby each Agister and the Steward have installed in their cars a two-way radio, enabling them to pass and receive messages from Police Control and also to communicate direct with each other. This is of tremendous benefit when an animal is injured in a road accident or is otherwise in trouble. The Police call up the Agister on the radio and within minutes he will be on the scene of the mishap.

Accidents on the road have decreased from 378 in 1962 to less than half that number today, due mainly to the fencing of some forest roads, but even so a considerable part of the Agisters' time is absorbed in dealing with these emer-gencies. Since the majority of road accidents occur after dark he frequently works under conditions of great difficulty. Of necessity each Agister is issued with a humane killer and when dealing with an injured animal he is authorised by the Verderers to use his own judgment in deciding whether or not to put the animal down.

During the summer months, when the animals have a smooth coat, the owners' brands are clearly visible but in winter the hair grows long and thick and brands can

1

seldom be seen. The Agister knows a great many of the ponies and cattle by sight and no problem arises in communicating with the owner in the event of trouble, but in other cases he has to round up the affected beast and, with special branding scissors, he clips the long hair over the brand thereby exposing it for recognition.

A further aid to identification is known as tail-marking. On the autumn drifts (round-ups) the tail is cut to a special shape; in the case of two of the Agisters one or two notches out of the right side and in the case of the third an all round cut near the top. These marks indicate that the owner of that particular animal lives in or adjacent to the area controlled by that Agister.

In addition to ensuring the welfare of animals under his control, each Agister has to collect for the Verderers the marking or grazing fees (as explained in a previous chapter). On receipt of the appropriate payment for cattle the Agister clips into the ear of the animal a plastic ear tag coloured according to the current year and this enables him, when seeing cattle in the Forest, to determine immediately whether the fee for the year has been paid. The same procedure cannot be followed for ponies because this causes unacceptable festering and no alternative visual mark has yet been found.

During the winter the amount of food available in the forest is necessarily restricted and the animals use their reserves of fat stored up in the summer. Nevertheless in the late winter many animals, both ponies and cattle, lose condition to an extent which renders it advisable for them to be returned to their owners' holdings. Local veterinary surgeons have formed an Advisory Panel and each winter month a veterinary surgeon, a Verderer and the Agister concerned examine all animals with a view to laying down a standard of condition to be adopted by the Agister during the ensuing month. The Agister causes any animal falling below this standard to be removed.

At all sittings of the Court of Verderers and on other special occasions such as the Stallion Show, the Agisters wear a most distinctive livery consisting of green jackets, riding breeches and leather gaiters, together with hard hats bearing the insignia of the Verderers' Stirrup.

An Agister's job demands not only toughness but also the ability to improvise, for he is constantly faced with new and unexpected emergencies requiring immediate action. An animal trapped in a bog is not unusual and rescue methods are fairly standardised but ponies have been found with their heads wedged between branches, legs entangled in wire, tins embedded over hooves, etc. all of which call upon resourcefulness of the man.

Agisters are almost invariably recruited from commoners who have spent their lives working with forest animals for theirs is not a job which could be picked up by a newcomer in a few months.

1 *Pony drifting.* [RF]
2 *Ponies in pound.* [RF]
3 *Clipping "out" for branding.* [RF]
4 *Agister branding a New Forest yearling.* [RF]

2

3

4

Eleven

The Foresters

HUGH INSLEY

Although the New Forest was not afforested (placed under forest laws) until about 1079 there are disputed records to show that as early as the reign of King Canute the area was hunted and that forest officers were appointed to look after it. The Foresters at that time were referred to as Lesthegend and later as Regarders.

Because the emphasis was upon the forest as a place in which to hunt rather than to grow trees, the records made during the early history of the Forest nearly always refer to the Keepers, whose job it was to safeguard the King's deer. The existence of Foresters at that time was recorded more by their transgressions against the King's deer than their activities in forestry. For instance, in 1271 a Steward of the Forest, Walter de Kanc, was reported to have taken one hart (red deer stag) and six bucks (male fallow deer). When the Verderers and Foresters who had obviously known of these activities were asked to report, they admitted that Walter and his friends had in fact taken over 500 deer. The Verderers and Foresters received reprimands but Walter, who was held to blame for all, received severe treatment. For the 500 deer he was fined £5 000 and for the other deer taken and destruction done to his bailiwick, he and his family were placed at the will of the King and Queen; in effect their lives and property were at the court's mercy.

Whatever woodland existed on the Forest during the eleventh century would have been natural woodland surviving from the effects of the Bronze Age and later inhabitants of the area. Before it became necessary to preserve and deliberately grow trees for timber, the job of the early Forester was probably one of guarding the natural timber against thieves and cutting what was required for the Crown's purposes.

The first record of enclosure for growing timber in the Forest is in a return made in 1438 by Henry Carter of Walhampton and Thomas Coke of Menestede (Minstead) to account for: 'money paid for enclosing 720 perches of wood and underwood at 4d the perch, and in making 3 gates to the said enclosure, with hinges, hooks, hasps, staples, locks and keys bought for the said gates'.

In 1535 during Henry VIII's reign, Godshill Coppice was recorded as a one hundred year old plantation of oak, thus showing that the Foresters had been actively growing oak since at least 1435.

Towards the end of the sixteenth century the use of the Forest as a royal hunting preserve began to decline but it was not until the importance of the Forest as a source of timber for the Royal Navy became realised that the Foresters for the first time began to share a place of equal importance with the Keepers. This was emphasised by the 1698 Act of William III, which begins:

'Forasmuch as the Woods and Timber, not only in the said New Forest, but in this Kingdom in general hath of late Years been much wasted and impaired, and the said Forest, that might be of great use and conveniency for the Supply of His Majesty's Royal Navy, is in Danger of being destroyed, if some speedy course be not taken, to restore and preserve the Growth of Timber there;'

This provided for the immediate enclosure and planting of 2 000 acres and 200 acres more to be enclosed yearly for twenty years. The Crown also took the power of rolling enclosure which was not ended until 1877.

The method of planting the oak woods after the 1698 Act is interesting in that they were sown, not planted as is the practice now. Three acorns were sown in each bed or spit and the spits were spaced a yard apart. Half a bushel of acorns was allotted for each forest worker to plant in a day by the Regarders, two of whom stayed on site to ensure that the work was done properly. After the acorns had been planted, hawes, holly berries, sloes and hazel nuts were planted throughout the area and traps were set by the Keepers to catch mice which would eat the acorns.

The Foresters and Keepers were the main people towards whom the penalties for abusing the Act were directed. A fine of £10 and being declared unemployable for life on Crown Estates was the penalty for cutting beech or oak trees, whilst for allowing a charcoal hearth within 1 000 paces of any Inclosure made under the Act, a Forester could be fined £100.

Despite these severe penalties the Foresters appear to have avoided their responsibilities. In 1789 their neglect "allowing constant thieving" is blamed for a lack of suitable oak trees for Royal Navy timber.

Following the Forestry (Transfer of Woods) Act 1923, the Forest was transferred to the Minister of Agriculture along with the Forest of Dean and the newly formed Forestry Commission was made responsible for their care and management. Forestry and the growing of timber tempered by the consideration for amenity – for the Forest was becoming a resort even then – remained the primary objective of the Foresters.

The New Forest Act 1949 made them responsible for a certain amount of open forest work also; this required the Forestry Commission to control scrub by cutting and burning and to carry out some drainage if considered reasonable and necessary and with the agreement of the Verderers.

The Foresters are responsible for the day to day management of the Forest. Today there are nine Foresters headed by three Head Foresters, each of whom controls a section of the Forest's economy. One section deals with all the felling, thinning, preparation and sale of timber whilst another controls the establishment and maintenance of new plantations as well as the open forest work. The third section is responsible for the recreation facilities in the Forest and the conservation of its fauna and flora. As such they are the first group of Foresters in Britain to work as a specialist recreation and conservation section. To assist them there are mechanical engineers who maintain the machinery all-important in modern forestry, and civil engineers who construct the forest roads and forest drains, as well as designing and constructing the car parks which are provided around all the car-free areas.

Through almost a thousand years of the New Forest's history the job of its Foresters has changed three times: from guardians of a hunting preserve valued only for its deer to timber growers whose efforts have conserved the woodlands as we know them today to their newest role as recreation managers dealing with this century's biggest growth industry – tourism. The new breed of Forester is a highly trained technician but fortunately those who take up this vocation never forget that care for the natural world that led them into it in the first place – and that in the end will save the New Forest and all our forests if we want it to.

1 *Felling an oak for the roof trusses of York Minster.* [GG]
2 *Planting.* [TR]

Twelve

The Forest Keepers

MICHAEL CLARKE

"You shall truly execute the Office of a Keeper of the King's wild beasts. You shall be of good behaviour yourself towards the King's wild beasts and the vert of the same Forest. You shall not conceal the office (offence) of any other person, either in vert or venison that shall be done within your charge . . ."

This oath of a forest keeper was recorded by Manwood in 1598. Nearly six hundred years earlier King Canute may have created the office of Tineman, who had much the same job.

Between the eleventh and seventeenth centuries the New Forest remained the hunting preserve of the Sovereigns of the day with the forest keepers tending the deer and enforcing the rigid forest laws.

Manwood records a law passed by King Edward the First . . . 'that if a man be apprehended hunting in the forest without warrant (permission) though he hath not taken a wild beast he shall be punished as if he hath taken and killed one.' Even so – according to Manwood – a poacher could only be im-

prisoned pending trial if he was 'Taken in the Manner' or caught red-handed as we would say today. He records four degrees of being Taken in the Manner:

Dog draw: Where a man has wounded a deer and followed it with hound or dog, drawing after it to recover it.
Stable stand: Found by a 'standing' ready to shoot deer, or with hounds ready to slip them after deer.
Back bare: Having killed a deer was found carrying it away.
Bloody hand: Found in suspicious circumstances with blood on him.

Unless taken in the manner and arrested, the Court of Attachment, if the offence was discovered by other means, could 'attach 'or distrain on an offender's goods or chattels to ensure his attendance at the next Forest Eyre. Hence the term Court of Attachment – the first Court before which offenders against the forest laws appeared.

1

During 1848 and 1849 much evidence was given before the Duncan Committee of the predations of deer onto the commoners' holdings. It was alleged that the numbers of deer in the forest had been as high as 7 000 or 8 000 but the actual numbers found by census were:

1845 – 4 582
1846 – 3 552
1847 – 3 196

from which it would appear that the numbers were already being reduced heavily. In 1850 a Royal Commission (the Portman Commission) was appointed and the Deer Removal Act of 1851 followed very closely the recommendations of that Commission. Its effect was to:

provide for the removal of the deer;
empower the Crown to enclose a further 10 000 acres for the growth of timber.

The Keepers made considerable efforts to implement this 'deer removal', but there was violent agitation by the commoners against the powers of enclosure given to the Deputy Surveyor and this resulted in the appointment of a Select Committee which made recommendations resulting in the passing of the New Forest Act 1877, laying the basis for the administration of the forest as we know it today. Evidence was given before the Select Committee proving that the unenclosed pastures of the forest had suffered by the drastic reduction in the numbers of deer. In 1883 G E Briscoe Eyre, a Verderer, records '. . . the value and extent of such pasture depends largely upon the number of species by which it is depastured'. Thus it was quickly recognised that the deer were important to the survival of the open forest lawns and though the Deer Removal Act remained in force until 1971 it ceased to be observed and the deer were saved from possible extermination.

The Keepers' duties today bring them more into contact with the many visitors to the Forest although the deer remain the focal point around which their year revolves.

The Forest is divided into two ranges, each in the charge of a Head Keeper who supervises the work of six beat Keepers. During April a census is taken of the deer on each beat, involving the Keepers in hours of patient observation. From this census a shooting plan is made, for the deer must be controlled to prevent numbers rising beyond the capacity of their winter food supply on the Forest; other factors to be considered include the vulnerable state of the young plantations and the likelihood of damage to neighbours' crops. Using high velocity rifles from specially-sited high seats the Keepers cull the deer in due season. During summer when roe buck are in season this can mean a working day starting at dawn and lasting into the late evening, since the deer lie up during the heat of the day and are most easily seen on their feeding grounds at dawn or dusk. Poaching continues to be a problem with deer grazing near the forest roads providing an easy target for the poacher using a car at night.

Regrettably animals other than deer have to be controlled, for the hare, rabbit and grey squirrel all damage the trees and if the Foresters' work is to succeed then the Keeper must keep their numbers in check.

The Keeper can be regarded as the Forest "policeman", patrolling his beat not only to check for infringements of the byelaws but also to monitor the many recreational activities merrily going on around him. He is particularly busy in spring and summer when his wildlife surveys and conservation work have to be fitted in between visits to car parks and picnic places to talk to members of the public.

The New Forest Keeper is a man who lives with the forest throughout the year, carrying on the tradition of caring for it as did the Tineman nearly a thousand years ago.

1 *Young fallow deer.* [RF] 2 *New Forest Keepers.* [HI]
2

Thirteen

New Forest ponies

DIONIS MACNAIR

In early times ponies roamed all over Britain but as farming and the population increased they were confined to small areas where they evolved slightly differently to suit local conditions and usages. In the New Forest they did all the work of the smallholdings, pulled the trap to market, carried the man to his work, and, within living memory, the children to school. Long ago they acquired a reputation as good children's ponies since James I is reputed to have had one for his children. They were always used to round up the cattle and ponies on the Forest and "colt hunting" is still not only a necessary part of the commoners' way of life but, along with pony racing, his traditional sport. This has encouraged the faster, sure-footed type of pony. When the New Forest Scouts were raised they were unusual among Yeomanry Regiments in being mounted on their own ponies who although small and rough had no difficulty in carrying the men and all their equipment Indeed, two of them managed to win the Auxiliary Services Jumping Competition at Tidworth Tattoo in 1902.

The earliest recorded attempt to improve the breed and get a larger faster pony was by the use of the thoroughbred "Masque", 1765–69. Thoroughbreds were also used on Forest mares by the Duke of York in attempting to breed for the Army. Some cart blood was doubtless used to get a heavier pony to haul timber and in 1852 the Office of Woods, thinking poorly of the ponies of the time, borrowed an Arab stallion from Prince Albert but he was not well patronised.

A persistent criticism has been that there were excellent mares who moved extraordinarily well but the standard of stallion was poor, so in 1891 the Society for the Improvement of New Forest Ponies was formed to award stallion premiums and hold annual races on Balmer Lawn. Lord Arthur Cecil considered the ponies inbred but decided that as all British ponies had a common derivation the thing to do was to bring stallions from another area and so breed a British pony. He brought to the Forest Welsh stallions with very Arab characteristics still seen particularly in the "Denny Danny" line, a black Highland pony with yellow eyes (witch eyes and the dun coat he also brought are found in the "Spitfire" line), some Fells and an Exmoor. A Polo Pony "Field Marshall" is the ancestor of many of today's best ponies; the last outcross allowed was a Dartmoor.

In 1938 the above-mentioned Society amalgamated with the Burley and District New Forest Pony and Cattle Society to form the New Forest Pony Breeding and Cattle Society and since then no outside blood has been permitted in Registered ponies. This has been possible because the New Forest Verderers can control which stallions run and will only allow suitable sound registered stallions onto the Forest. Since 1970 all stallions must hold a Veterinary Certificate. So although a commoner may turn out any mare, provided her colts are removed before they are old enough to breed (many do this: piebalds and skewbalds are never pure bred Foresters), it is possible to breed pedigree stock on the Open Forest, unlike common land elsewhere where there are no Verderers.

The environment, aided by efforts to supply the current market, has a decisive effect in producing a type. For example the small carthorse is no longer needed so the heavy, hairy-heeled pony has practically disappeared. Nowadays the ponies are used mainly as children's or family ponies; they are very versatile, fast for their size, hardy and good tempered. They usually jump and several have achieved British Show Jumping Association standard. Many are to be found in various Pony Club teams around the country. Whilst narrow and docile enough for small or disabled children, they are strong enough for mother to ride. Few are afraid of traffic, often their undoing on the unfenced Forest roads but essential when ridden or driven. Now that as many New Forest ponies are bred on private studs as in the Forest, owners who favour a particular type can usually find it among the mixed ancestry and by selective breeding accentuate it again to diversify the type.

Colt hunting has two forms: one where perhaps two people ride out to catch an individual pony and secondly "drifts" held in late summer and autumn and organised by the Verderers' Agisters. A number of commoners ride over an area and drive as many ponies as possible into a pound. Here, the pounded ponies are wormed to free them from parasites and those to be sold or wintered on the holdings are loaded into lorries and trailers.

The original pony sale was at Lyndhurst Fair on Swan Green but as road traffic increased it moved to its present site near Beaulieu Road Station. Sales are held in April, August, September, October and November. From September the sales are predominately of foals, mainly colts. First to be sold are those ponies eligible for registration as New Forest ponies, then the registered ones and finally those not eligible. Riding horses and ponies are sold in a separate ring in the afternoon. The Fair atmosphere still prevails and there is always the chance of a bargain: one colt foal sold for 15 gns to a gentleman as a present for his granddaughter turned out a top class jumper and was eventually sold for £1 500! In the first year of the Pony Society's Performance Competition four of the ten prize winners were bought as foals at these sales.

To buy a wild sucker and turn it, four years later, into a satisfactory child's pony can be most rewarding but it can also be frustrating and time-consuming. Taken from its dam and familiar surroundings the foal will at first do all it can to get back to the Forest, so it must be securely shut in where it cannot hurt itself until it gets to know and trust its new owners. Often it will not eat, or only eat soft hay and long grass laboriously cut for it; teaching it will require much patience. As ponies are herd animals who hate being alone two foals usually do better than one.

The Forest as it appears today has been made and kept by the browsing and grazing of the ponies, cattle and deer. The pony's role is vital, as it lives not only on grass but on gorse, which has great food value but requires horny tongues and hairy faces to cope with it, brambles, holly, ivy and heather. He stores fat in the summer to use in the lean early months of the year. He is part of an ancient heritage but has adapted to all the various uses man has found for him and is now being exported to the continent where riding for children is becoming popular. Formerly continental children only started to ride when big enough to manage a horse but now there are over 5 000 New Forest ponies in Holland and many more in France, Germany and Scandinavia. Everywhere they have proved good tempered and teachable and so have made themselves new friends.

When you come to the Forest please do not feed the ponies, this draws them to the roads where they cause accidents to themselves and others.

1 *Beaulieu Road pony sales.* [RF]

1

Fourteen

Explore the Forest with maps

DONN SMALL

During an earlier administration the Forest was divided into nine Bailiwicks, each under the control of an honorary Master Keeper; they in turn appointed the groom-keepers who were responsible for fifteen Keepers' Walks covering the whole Forest. These walks are shown on Driver's map of 1789 which is reproduced on pages 2 and 3 of this book and also appear in name only on modern maps.

We have used the Walks as convenient divisions for the gazetteer which follows. Each has a map and a brief description to help the visitor decide where he wants to go. Every walk has its own character, from the heathland solitude of Ashley Walk to the ancient deer-haunted woodlands of Bolderwood.

This Forest is well endowed with both major and minor county roads from which all the forest car parks are easily accessible, as are the camping sites. The Commission has usually named the car parks after a local place name which is generally recorded on the map.

The reader is invited to choose from the small key map the particular Walk he wishes to visit, travel there by the appropriate county road, select a car park and from there, using the two and a half inch maps, follow the tracks of his choice. Long or short walks are possible within a particular Walk and some guidance is given below on the interpretation of the map symbols.

Private land within the Forest is clearly designated and walkers are advised to remain on the public footpaths as shown. All Statutory Inclosures are named, with boundaries shown as a solid grey line, usually indicating a bank and ditch. All tracks are either depicted by a single dotted line, or a double dotted line where vehicles have used them in the past. Within the Inclosures certain forest rides are gravelled for the purpose of timber haulage and emergency access to fires. They have been added to the Ordnance Survey maps to offer the walker

1

a dry surface and a well-identified route to follow. Unofficial access by cars is not permitted. The wide gates to Inclosures are often locked for security reasons but a wicket gate is usually provided alongside for man and horse. On the Open Forest Waste access is either by a path shown as a single dotted line often labelled FP: footpath or a track shown as double dotted lines, sometimes gravelled by the Forestry Commission.

Most forest bogs are impassable and they should be avoided. They are often named Bog, Flash or Bottom. There are sometimes prepared crossings often depicted as "FB", ie footbridge; "passage", ie a culverted gravel ridge; and "ford" usually crossable in summer but not in the winter unless the walker is adequately shod.

Unfenced highways are not often distinguishable from forest tracks, but an additional colour has been used to denote them. The railway can be crossed by bridge at points indicated. There are also cattle creeps under the A31, A35 and A337 and these can be used by walkers to avoid the risk of crossing major traffic routes. They have been specially added to the maps.

A full legend to all Ordnance Survey details on these maps is included on page 116.

2

4

1 *By car: Knightwood Oak car park.* [TH]
2 *Fishing: Cadman's Pool.* [TH]
3 *Walking: bridge at Aldridgehill.* [TH]
4 *Walking: rest and picnic.* [TH]
5 *Camping: Hollands Wood campsite.* [TH]
6 *Riding: pony trekking on the heath.* [RF]

5

3

6

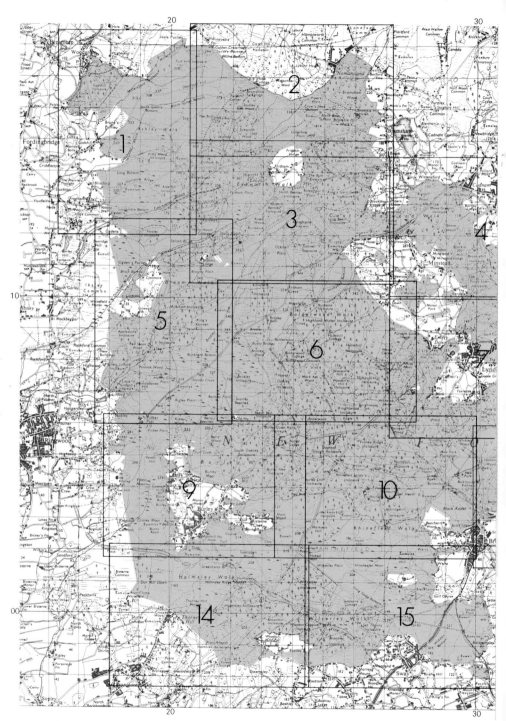

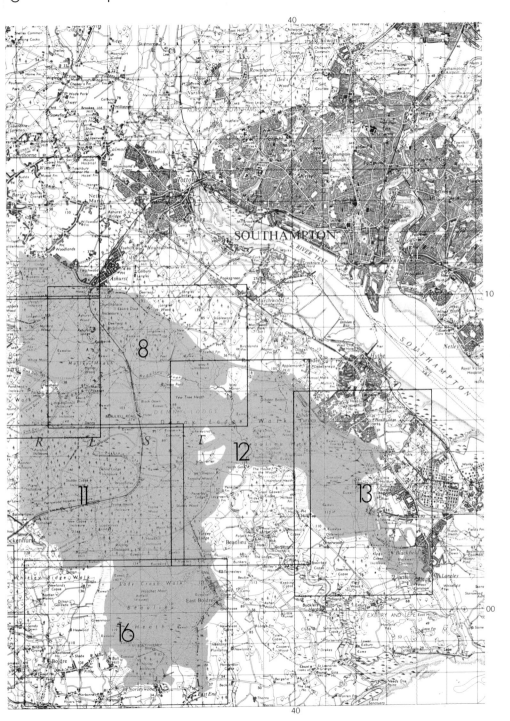

1

ASHLEY WALK

Named after the ash trees located around an old keeper's lodge at Lodge Hill this Walk covers the north west limits of the Forest, overlooking the River Avon. Large tracts of heathland are found in Stone Quarry Bottom, Hampton Ridge and Black Gutter Bottom. Two island Inclosures, Hasley and Pitts Wood, intrude into this otherwise treeless open space. Pitts Wood Inclosure was named after John Pitt, a Surveyor General of the Forest in 1773.

A notable feature of the stream banks in these valleys is the soil profile, valued by geologists in determining the past history of these deposits. Castle Hill near Godshill is said to be the only likely relic of a Norman fortification in the Forest.

Car parks will be found at Godshill, Castle Hill, Millersford, Godshill Cricket Pitch,

Abbot's Well, Ogdens, Dead Man's Hill, some affording fine views and others access on to foot tracks into the interior of the largest area in the Forest freed from cars and camping.

Interesting long walks using the map as a guide are from Cockley car park up to Lodge Hill via Pitts Wood across Ditchend Brook via Godshill Ridge. And from Abbot's Well car park via Hampton Ridge to the Ashley Cross tumulus thence westwards to Alder Hill Inclosure and Ogdens Farm. These Walks will depict some of the range of wildlife activity of these open heathlands. The forest gravelled roads in Godshill Inclosure are linked by grass rides, offering the walker a complete change of scenery.

The adjoining commons such as Hyde and Gorley, to the west, are not administered by the Forestry Commission.

1

2

1 *Black Gutter Bottom.* [HA]
2 *View through pine across Millersford Bottom.* [HA]
3 *Hover-fly.* [RF]
4 *Ling on Hampton Ridge heath.* [HA]
5 *Grey squirrel.* [TH]
6 *Common gorse.* [RF]
7 *Fairy Shrimps – a forest rarity.* [HA]

3

4

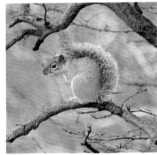

5

6

7

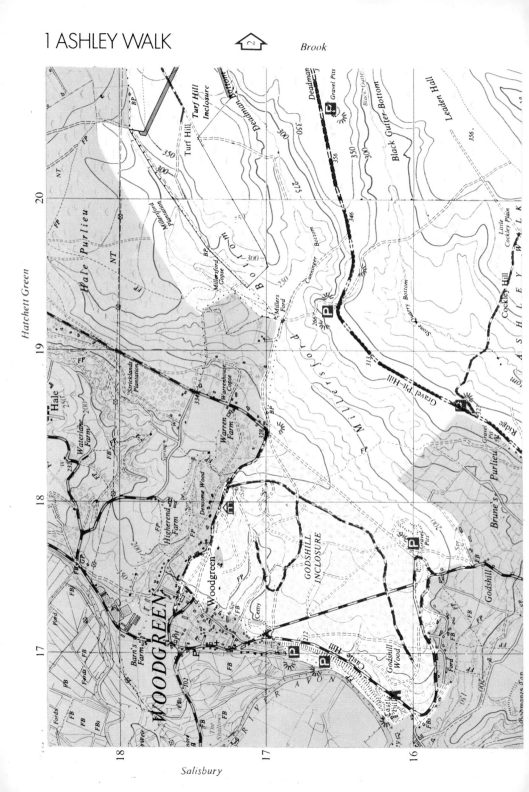

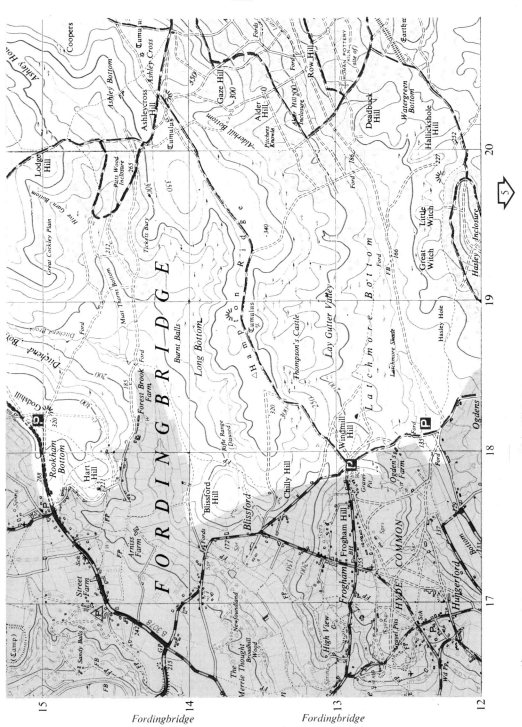

2 BRAMBLE HILL WALK

Named after the small bramble covered woodland west of Bramshaw this most northerly part of the Forest is one of contrasts between the beautiful old Bramshaw Wood, the wet Howen Bottom and the oak plantations in Islands Thorns Inclosure. The original Groom Keeper's Lodge was at Bramble Hill which is now a private hotel. Here the Groom Keeper fed the wild deer with holly, ash and hay. It was said that, before the woodlands matured, from the hill one could see Southampton and the Isle of Wight on a clear day. At Bramshaw Telegraph during the Napoleonic Wars, semaphore was used in a link of communications from London to Plymouth.

Car parks will be found at Bramshaw Telegraph, Turf Hill, Longcross Pond, Coppice of Linwood, and in the winter Piper's Wait which is the highest point in the Forest being 420 feet above sea level; this is a small caravan site from April until September. An interesting long walk from Bramshaw Telegraph southwards into Islands Thorns Inclosure will lead the walker to an early earth castle at Studley and via the many grass rides to the solitude within the oak and beech plantations. Bramshaw Wood, a very mature ancient and ornamental wood, affords the walker some of the sylvan splendours of beechwoods sloping down to Judds Hill, as does Eyeworth Wood which is dealt with separately in the Eyeworth Walk. Longcross Pond is a fine representative of the Forest manmade dewponds which are seldom dry and provide valuable watering places for forest animals and birds. Access into Coppice of Linwood Inclosure can be gained from the car park south east of Longcross Pond.

1

2

1 *Crow's Nest Bottom.* [HA]
2 *Wood mouse.* [HA]
3 *Sulphur fungus.* [HA]
4 *Longcross Pond at sunset.* [TH]
5 *Hard fern.* [HA]

3

4

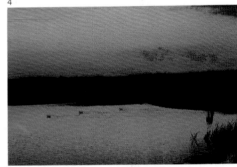

5

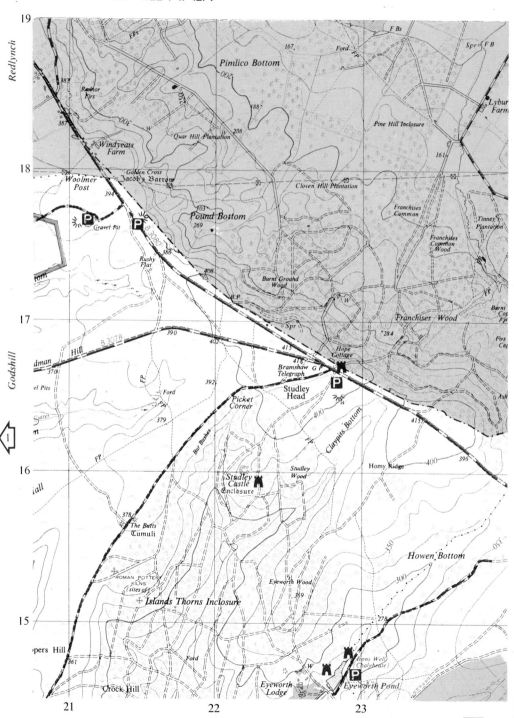

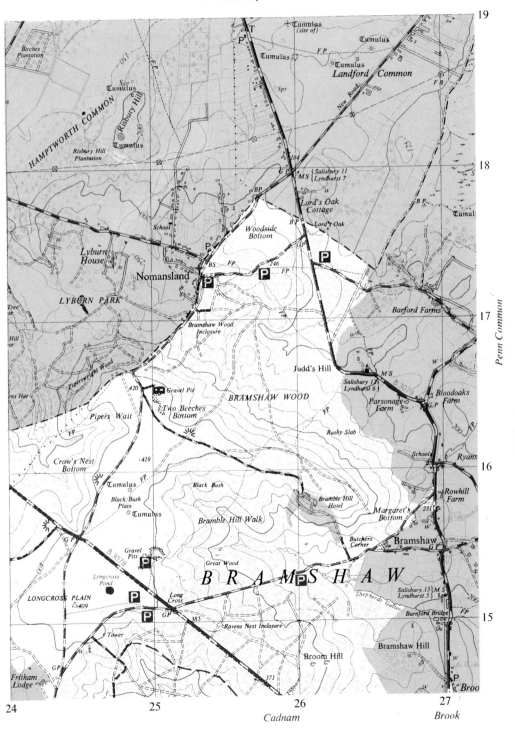

3

EYEWORTH WALK

One of the pleasant features of this Walk is the Pond which was created for the storage of water to assist in the manufacture of gunpowder near to the former Groom's Lodge which is now a private residence. This Walk covers a great variety of forest assets from Ancient and Ornamental Woodlands such as Eyeworth, Anses and White Shoot Bottom Woods, to the beautiful Inclosures of Amberwood, Slodens, Ocknell, the Bentleys, Broomy, Hollyhatch, Longbeech, Kings Garn Gutter and the great open level ground of Stoney Cross Plain resulting from the 1939–45 wartime airfield. The origin of the word "Garn" or Garden is understood to be where the Royal beehives were placed in the early days. Streams in the north of the forest are termed "gutters" or "brooks", and in the south they are called "waters".

Notable historical features are the Butt – a fine bronze age burial tumulus; Ocknell Clump – where in 1775 Scots Pine was reintroduced to the Forest and especially used for demarcating Inclosure boundaries. Today can be seen how profusion of natural seedlings from these trees changes the open nature of the forest scenery and examples of complete clearance will be seen where the Forestry Commission is attempting to re-establish the open forest character. Certain clumps of pine are retained as natural landscape features.

Car parks will be found at Eyeworth Pond, Fritham Oak, Janesmoor Pond, Longbeech, Stoney Cross, South Bentley, Anses Wood, Cadmans, Ocknell and Foxhill Ponds, each giving access to Inclosures, or heathland or restful waterside picnic places, or open spaces over which to play cricket, fly kites, etc. Toilets are provided at Stoney Cross car park.

Camping is available at Longbeech and Ocknell from April to September with special overflow provisions during Bank Holiday weekends at Ocknell Pond and North Bentley.

1

2

3

6

4

7

8

1 *Eyeworth Pond.* [HA]
2 *Oak for the future – South Bentley Inclosure.* [RF]
3 *Eyeworth Wood.* [HA]
4 *Common frog.* [HA]
5 *Longbeech camp site.* [RF]
6 *Bogbean.* [HA]
7 *Fox.* [FC]
8 *King's Garn Gutter Inclosure from the air, 1971.*
[FC]

5

59

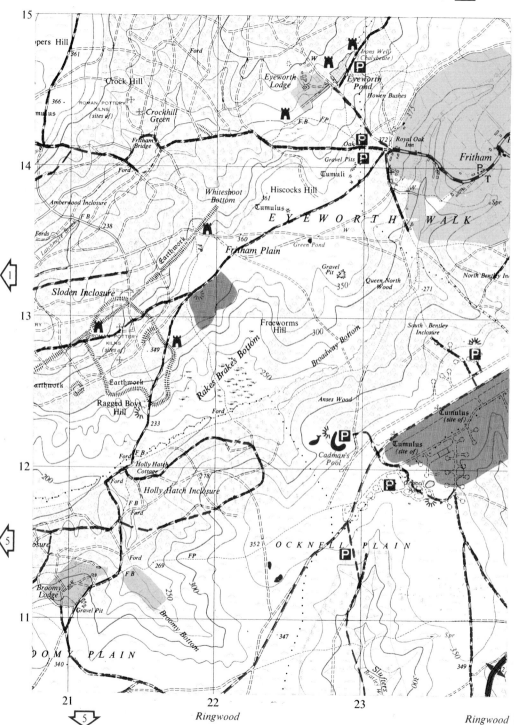

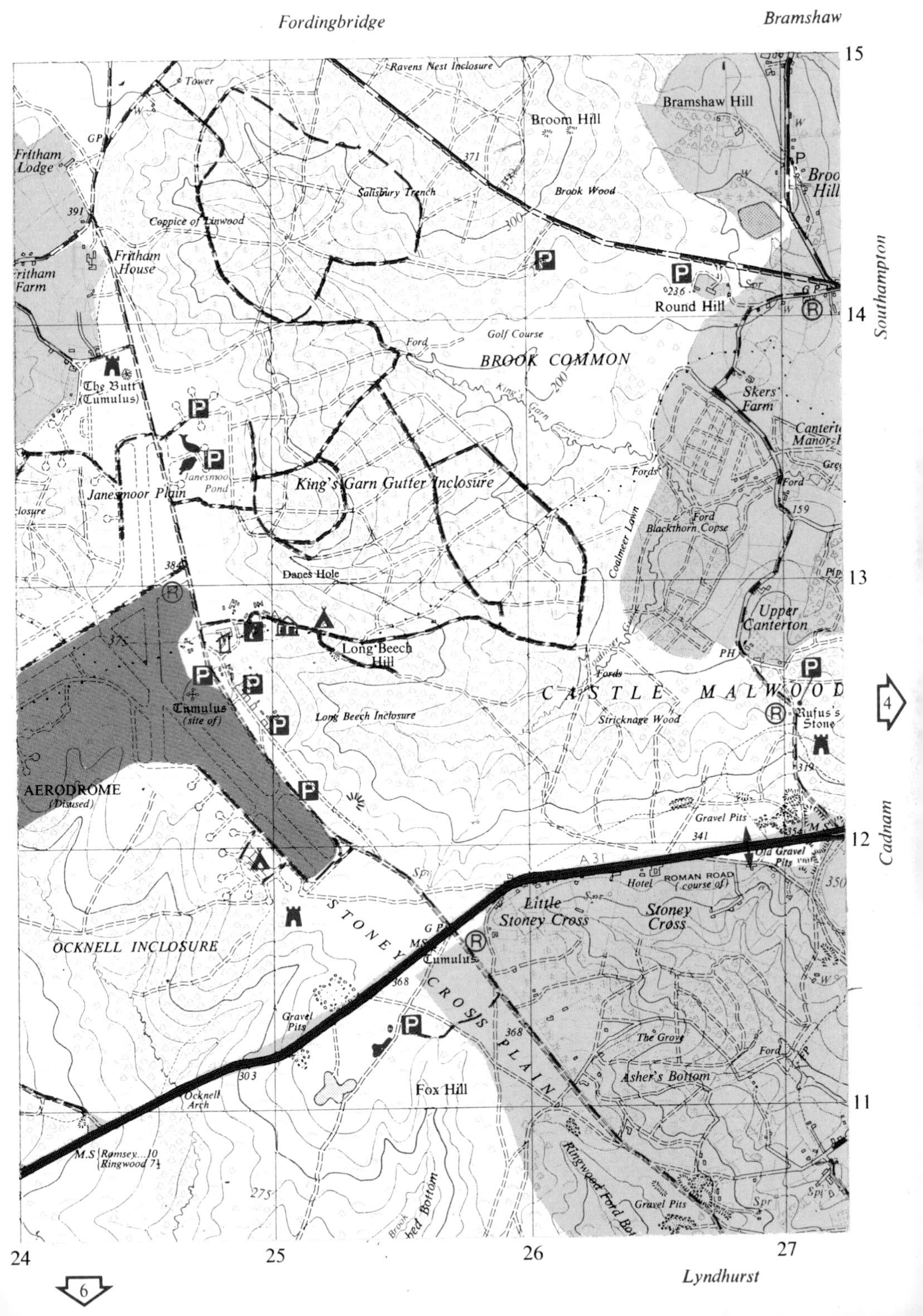

15

Tower

Ravens Nest Inclosure

Bramshaw Hill

Broom Hill

Broo Hill

Fritham
Lodge

GP

391

Coppice of Linwood

Salisbury Trench

Brook Wood

371

Fritham
House

ritham
Farm

The Butt
(Tumulus)

P

Golf Course

Ford

BROOK COMMON

P

P

Round Hill

Southampton

14

R

GP

Skers'
Farm

Cantert
Manors

P

King's Garn Gutter Inclosure

Janesmoor
Pond

Janesmoor Plain

losure

Fords

Greg

Ford

159

Coalmeer Lawn

Ford
Blackthorn Copse

13

384

Danes Hole

Upper
Canterton

R

Fords

PH

Long Beech
Hill

CASTLE MALWOOD

P

P

Long Beech Inclosure

Stricknage Wood

R

Rufus's
Stone

Tumulus
(site of)

319

P

AERODROME
(Disused)

Gravel Pits

341

Old Gravel
Pits

12

Cadnam

A 31

350

Hotel

ROMAN ROAD
(course of)

4

STONEY

Little
Stoney Cross

Stoney
Cross

OCKNELL INCLOSURE

GP

MS

R

Tumulus

CROSS

368

The Grove

Ford

Gravel
Pits

P

Asher's Bottom

303

368

Ocknell
Arch

PLAIN

Fox Hill

11

M.S Romsey...10
Ringwood 7½

275

Gravel Pits

Spr

Spi

24

25

26

27

6

4

CASTLE MALWOOD WALK

Overlapping with Eyeworth and Bramble Hill Walk, this Walk was created for the large Master Keeper's lodge at Castle Malwood, where it is alleged William Rufus spent the night before his death. Castle Malwood and Bramble Hill Walks combine to form the northern Bailiwick. Today the Lodge, rebuilt, is divided into private residential flats close to the great iron-age fort at Running Hill.

Through this Walk runs the London–Plymouth trunk road, its traffic volume swollen by the M27 motorway. Thus the Walk is divided by this trunk road and to its north is the most visited place in the Forest – Rufus Stone. Access to remnants of woodland is from the Brook road into a beautiful ancient and ornamental wood, Bignell. From the Cadnam inter-change the main artery to the capital of the Forest, Lyndhurst, is the A337 which passes through some lovely heathland and woodland. Car parks at Shave Green offer access to the Shave Green Inclosures and the minor road to Minstead offers occasional stopping places to Hazel and Brockishill Woods.

Provision is being made for car park access to Busketts Lawn and Ironshill Inclosures and the beautiful enclosed forest lawns of Busketts Wood. Limited access is possible from the Ashurst Forest Office on the A35 and from woodlands to the north of Ashurst.

Visitors may be interested in the details of the original Rufus Stone compared to the iron casing of today. The Rufus Stone was a three-sided stone pillar erected in 1745 by John, Lord Delaware, when he was Master Keeper at Bolderwood Lodge, to perpetuate the memory of the death of William Rufus (King William II) which by legend occurred at Canterton Glen, although recent doubts about this location are discussed in Chapter 6. The inscription placed on the Stone, which is given below, embroiders the plain facts which have come down to us. The Anglo Saxon Chronicle does not mention

an oak nor Tirel nor that the King was struck on the breast. The spelling of Tirel is also different from that accepted today, but standard spellings are a comparatively recent development.

The inscription reads:

"Here stood the Oak Tree on which an arrow shot by Sir Walter Tyrrell at a stag glanced and struck King William II surnamed Rufus on the breast of which stroke he instantly died on the second day of August anno 1100.
King William II being thus slain was laid on a cart belonging to one Purkess and drawn from hence to Winchester, and buried in the Cathedral Church of that City. That the spot where an event so memorable happened might not hereafter be unknown this Stone was set up by John, Lord Delaware, who has seen the tree growing in this place."

Later the following inscriptions were added to the Stone but were lost when the present iron casing was added:

"This spot was visited by King George III and Queen Charlotte on the twenty-seventh of June, MDCCLXXXIX."
"This Stone was repaired by John Richard Earl Delaware anno 1789."

The Stone was attacked by relic-hunting vandals, and it was found necessary to place the present iron casing over it bearing the original inscriptions slightly amended as well as the following one:

"This Stone having been much mutilated and the inscriptions on each of the three sides been defaced, this more durable memorial with the original inscription was erected, in the year 1841 by William Sturges Bourne, Warden."

1 *Stricknage Wood.* [RF]
2 *New Forest cicada.* [RF]
3 *Ocknell Clump – first planting of Scots pine in the New Forest in 1775.* [RF]
4 *Rufus Stone.* [TR]
5 *Purple loosestrife.* [HA]

1

2

4

5

3

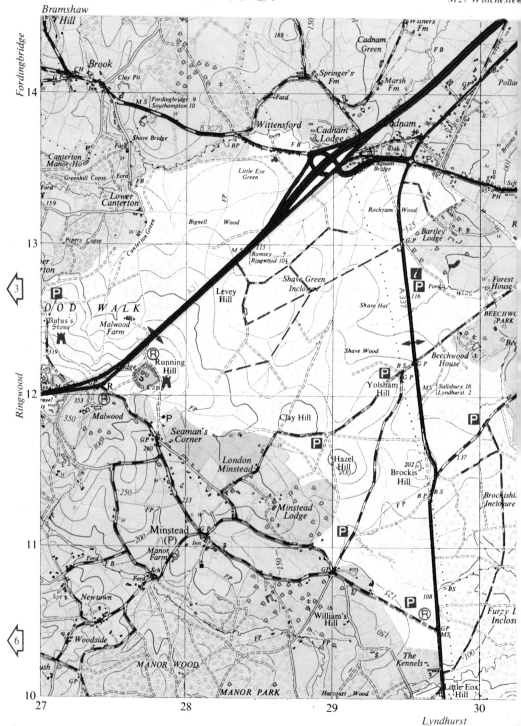

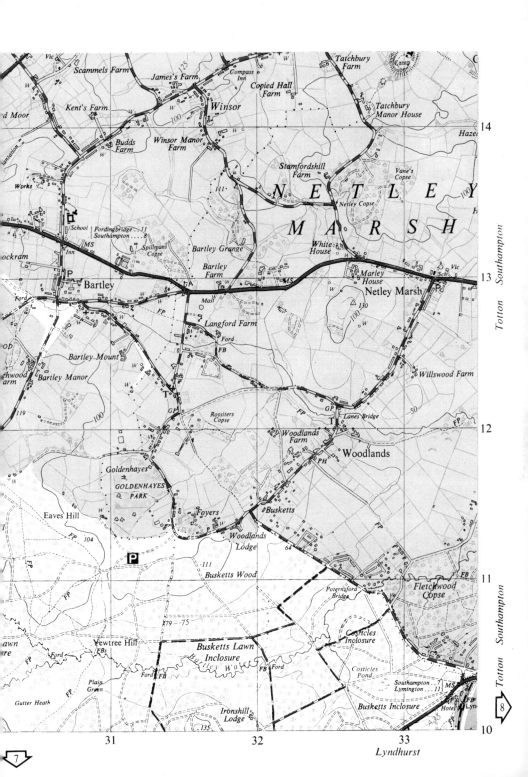

5

BROOMY WALK

Forming part of the west boundary, believed to have been named after the birch and broom thickets in the oak heath, this Walk has some very diverse woodlands both unenclosed and enclosed.

The main stream courses of Dockens Water and Linford Brook flow from the northeast to the southwest bound for the River Avon through Forest lawns. They provide good wet pastures on the open forest and shaded woody corridors especially in Milkham and Roe Inclosures where stream life abounds.

One of the notable historic features of this Walk is the infamous smugglers' road along which illicit goods were conveyed from Christchurch and Mudeford to Winchester. A good description of these activities will be found in Chapter 7. A traditional historic royal bee-hive garden will be seen at King's Garden, now a reseeded lawn on the east side of Roewood Inclosure and still valued by today's beekeepers. Extensive earthworks can be traced amidst the trees in the centre of Roe Inclosure.

Car parks will be found at Linford Bottom with access to picnic places on the stream banks and paddling in gravel-bottomed streams. Appleslade Inclosure offers extensive varied walks and scenery; Milkham Inclosure has a great diversity of natural wildlife within the Inclosure, which can be witnessed when following the forest rides. Using the map many long and varied walks can be undertaken particularly to Pinnick and Red Shoot Woods where a variety of plant life can be seen during the seasons.

1 *Broad-bordered Bee Hawk moth.* [RF]
2 *Foxgloves.* [RF]
3 *Amberwood Inclosure in autumn.* [RF]
4 *Linford Bottom.* [RF]
5 *Dockens Water.* [HA]
6 *Slufters Pond.* [RF]
7 *Broomy Inclosure oak – planted 1829.* [HA]

3
4
6
5
7

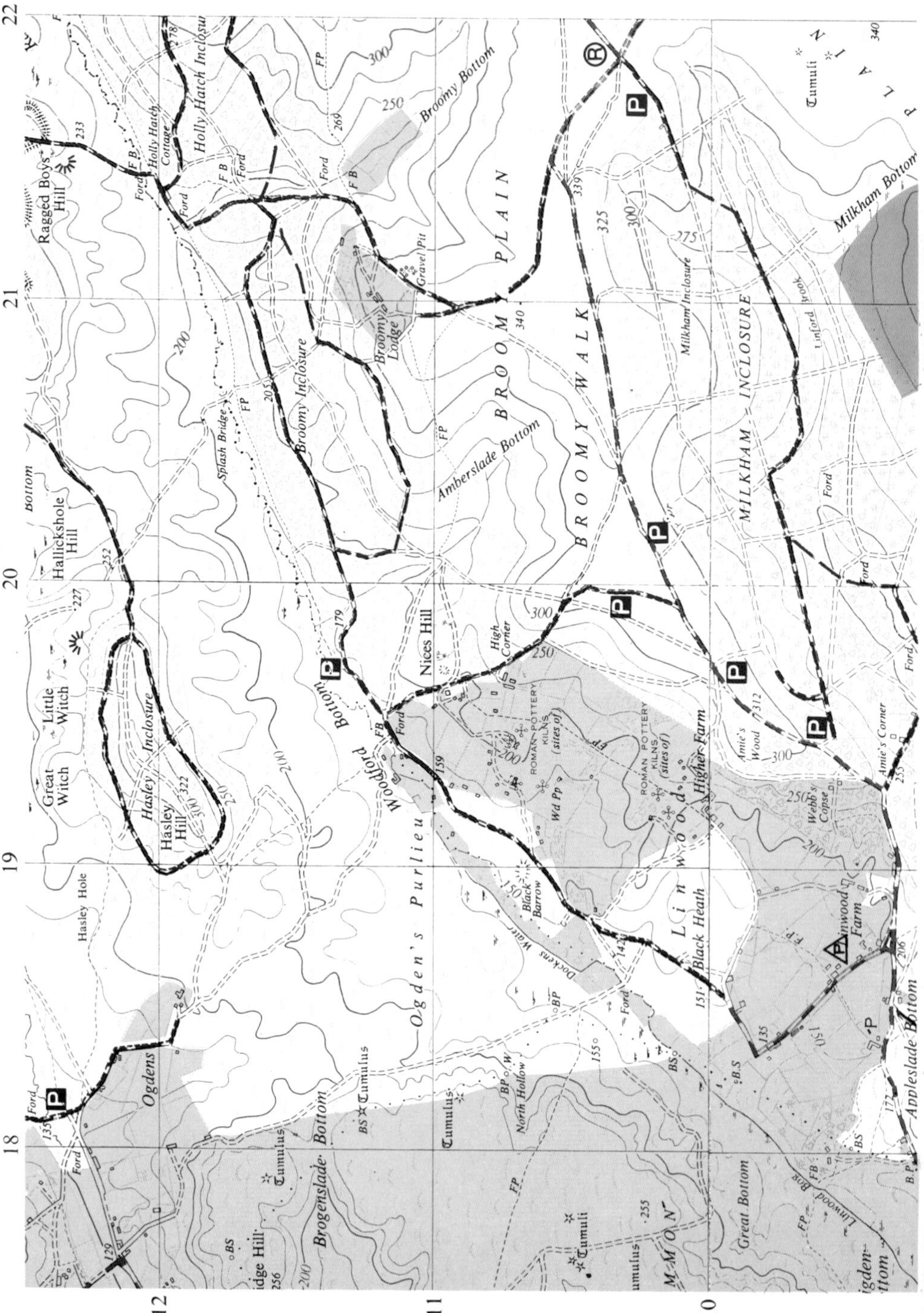

Ragged Boys Hill

Holly Hatch Cottage

Holly Hatch Inclosure

Ford   F B   Ford

Broomy Bottom

Gravel Pit

Broomy Lodge

Broomy Inclosure

Splash Bridge

Hallickshole Hill

Bottom

Great Witch

Little Witch

Hasley Inclosure

Hasley Hill 322

Hasley Hole

Nices Hill

High Corner

BROOM PLAIN

BROOMY WALK

MILKHAM INCLOSURE

Milkham Bottom

Milkham Inclosure

Longford Brook

Amerslade Bottom

Amie's Wood 312

Amie's Corner

Roman Pottery Kilns (sites of)

Higher Farm

Webby Copse

L i n w o o d s

Black Barrow

Black Heath

Docker's Water

Linwood Farm

Woodford Bottom

Ogden's Purlieu

Ogdens

Brogenslade Bottom

Ridge Hill

North Hollow

BS   Tumulus

Tumuli

Great Bottom

Appleslade Bottom

Ogden Bottom

Igden Bottom

C O M M O N

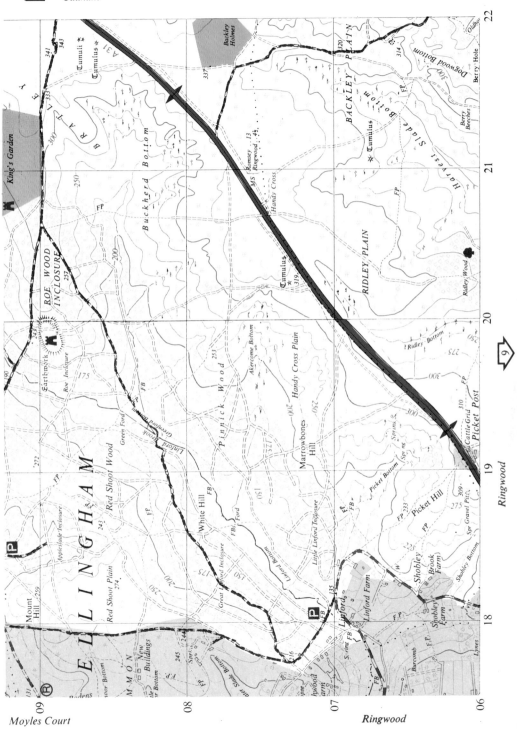

6

BOLDERWOOD WALK

This Walk situated in the central highland south of the A31 takes its name from the Master Keeper's Lodge pulled down in 1833 near to the present Keeper's Cottage. "Bolde" is an old English word for house. One of the main features of this Walk is the stand of giant Douglas Fir planted in the old Lodge grounds in 1859, and the adjoining arboretum and deer sanctuary. Other equally attractive features are the extensive woodlands, through which the energetic walker may step back into the past and see the oldest pollarded tree in the Forest, the Knightwood Oak.

Ancient scenic woodlands will be found at Bratley, Backley and Mark Ash Wood with the intervening valleys of Bushy Bratley, Blackensford Bottom and Highland Water, all of which are accessible by forest tracks.

Near Millyford Bridge will be seen the recently restored Portuguese Fireplace, a relic of 1914–1918 war buildings occupied by Portuguese troops. The Eagle Oak, a very mature oak, is where the last white-tailed eagle was shot in 1810. Backley Holms is a wartime reseeded lawn where wildlife and ponies often share early morning grazing. Access from the A31 has now been restricted for safety reasons.

Car parks are situated at Mogshade, where a simple oak cross erected on 14 April 1946 commemorates the presence of 3rd Canadian Division of RCASC in the Forest. From here access to an extensive forest road system within Highland Water Inclosure can be made. Bolderwood Green is well situated for the Forestry Commission's waymarked walks, including the Earl of Radnor's Memorial Stone, Moorsbarrow, Knightwood Oak and No Man's Walk, all associated with scenic woodlands and the historic old pollarded trees.

Near the small car park at Holidays Hill Cottage is a collection of forest reptiles which can be seen and studied in safety. On the Bolderwood–Emery Down road will be found the Highland Water viewpoint car park and a delightful series of small woodland car parks in settings offering a variety of scenery and walks into unenclosed woodlands. Small car parks at Acres Down give access to the north part of Highland Water Inclosure and the energetic will be rewarded by reaching Puckpits Inclosure, the home of some very tall mature conifer trees.

Camping is confined to a small informal site at Holidays Hill.

1 *Mark Ash Wood.* [RF]
2 *Detail from Radnor Stone.* [FC]
3 *Fallow deer.* [HA]
4 *Bolderwood Douglas firs and natural regeneration.* [HA]
5 *Roman bridge, Holidays Hill.* [RF]
6 *Rose Chafer.* [RF]
7 *Mark Ash Wood.* [RF]

1

2

3

5
6

7

4

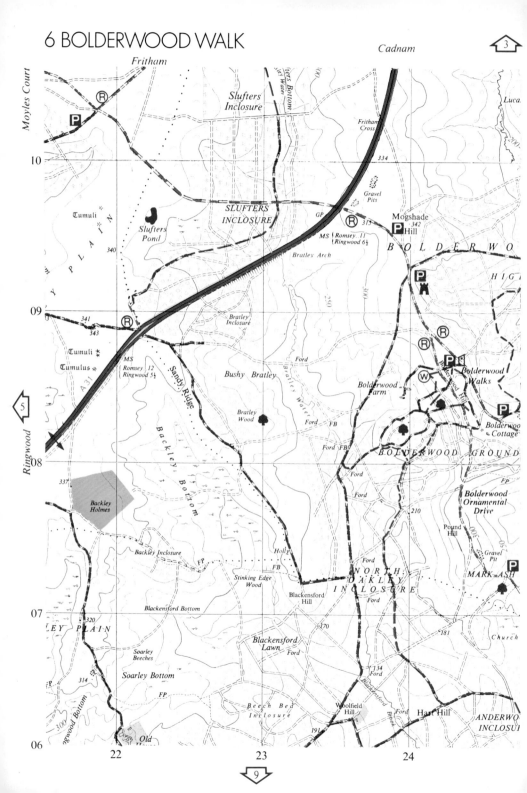

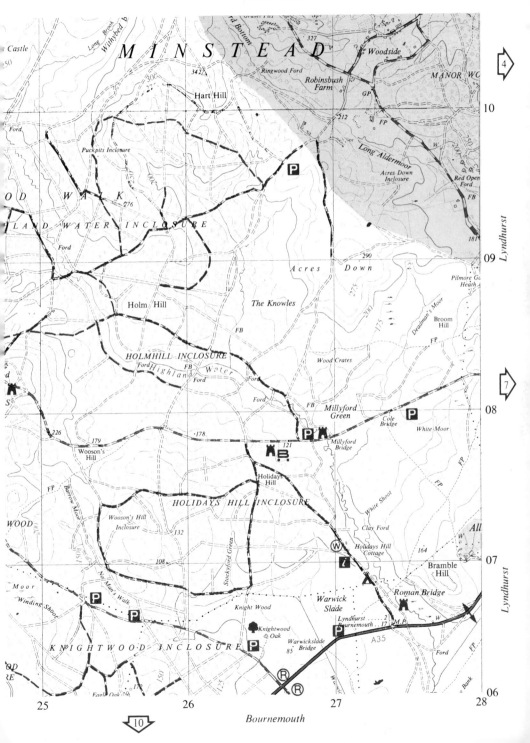

MINSTEAD

Castle

Long Brook Withybed b

327

Woodside

Ringwood Ford

342△

Hart Hill

Robinsbush Farm

MANOR WO

300

GP

Ford

212

Puckpits Inclosure

FP

276

Long Aldermoor

10

OD WALK

ILAND WATER INCLOSURE

Acres Down Inclosure

Red Open Ford

FB

181

Ford

Acres   Down

09

Holm Hill

The Knowles

Pilmore Ga Heath

Deadman's Moor

Broom Hill

FB

FP

HOLMHILL INCLOSURE

Ford Highland Water

FB

Wood Crates

FB Ford

Ford

Ford

226

179

·178

Wooson's Hill

121

FB

Millyford Green

Cole Bridge

White Moor

08

Millyford Bridge

B

HOLIDAYS HILL INCLOSURE

Holidays Hill

FP

White Shoot

FP

Clay Ford

WOOD

Wooson's Hill Inclosure

·132

White Shoot

108

Stockford Green

W

Holidays Hill Cottage

164

Bramble Hill

07

Moor

Winding Shoot

No Man's Walk

Knight Wood

Warwick Slade

Roman Bridge

KNIGHTWOOD INCLOSURE

Knightwood Oak

Warwickslade Bridge

85

Lyndhurst ..... 2 Lyndhurst Bournemouth . 17 M.P.

A35

Ford

Bank

06

Eagle Oak

25   26   27   28

7

IRONSHILL WALK

The centrepiece of this walk is the village of Lyndhurst, capital of the New Forest. Formerly a Royal manor, its name derives from old English meaning hillock of lime trees; the Queen's House, largely rebuilt in the seventeenth century, was the Manor house; the Verderers' Hall, mostly Tudor, adjoins it. Surrounding Lyndhurst are delightful open spaces such as Whitemoor; Bolton's Bench, named after Lord Bolton, a Lord Warden of the Forest in 1688; and Matley Heath, interspersed with woodland of all ages, including Rushpole, Bramble Hill, Janeshill and Matley Woods.

The most notable of the Inclosures are Pondhead and Park Ground which were early fields sown with oak in 1810, Ironshill where it is believed ironstone was worked, and Denny Inclosure which contains some early relics of mature beechwoods.

Interesting early earthworks can be seen at the Park Pale, or The Ridge, which encircled in 1291 an early, two hundred acre royal deer park south-east of Lyndhurst, later to be replaced in 1670 by Charles II by creation of "New Park" near Brockenhurst.

This walk is well served by county roads radiating from Lyndhurst, off which are forest car parks offering walks of all lengths and varied scenery, from heathland at Bolton's Bench and Matley Bridge to old woodland at Janeshill, Whitemoor and Denny Wood. There are some buildings around Lyndhurst worthy of mention: delightful thatched cottages at Swan Green, small forest dwellings at Gritnam Village and mellow Stuart symmetry of Queen's House, viewed from Shrubbs Hill Road. The Queen's House is the seat of the Deputy Surveyor, the Forestry Commission's chief officer in the Forest, and his staff.

Camping is confined to Matley and Denny Woods, good centres for exploring on foot the great mass of Inclosure woodland to the west and south. The Girl Guide Centre is at Foxlease south of Lyndhurst off the A337.

1

2

1 *Giant lacewing.* [RF]
2 *Lyndhurst – cricket on Swan Green.* [TH]
3 *Park Hill, Lyndhurst.* [HA]
4 *The Queen's House.* [SKY-VIEWS]
5 *Pondhead Inclosure oak – planted 1810.* [RF]

4

3

5

7 IRONS HILL WALK

Cadnam

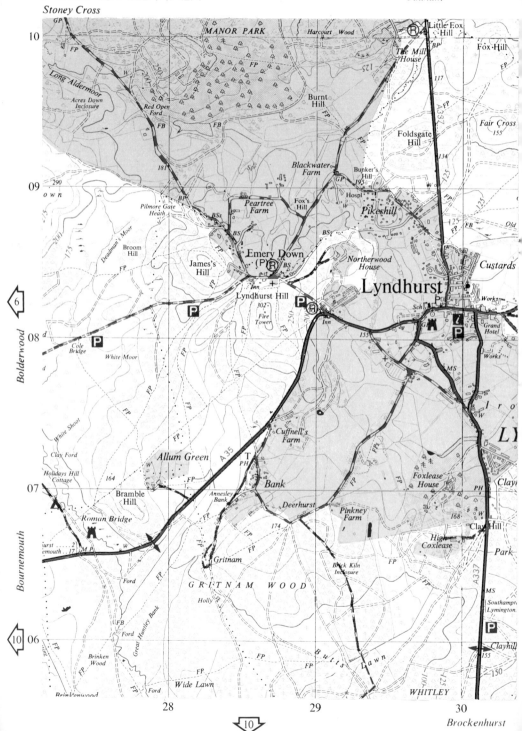

Stoney Cross

Bolderwood

Bournemouth

Brockenhurst

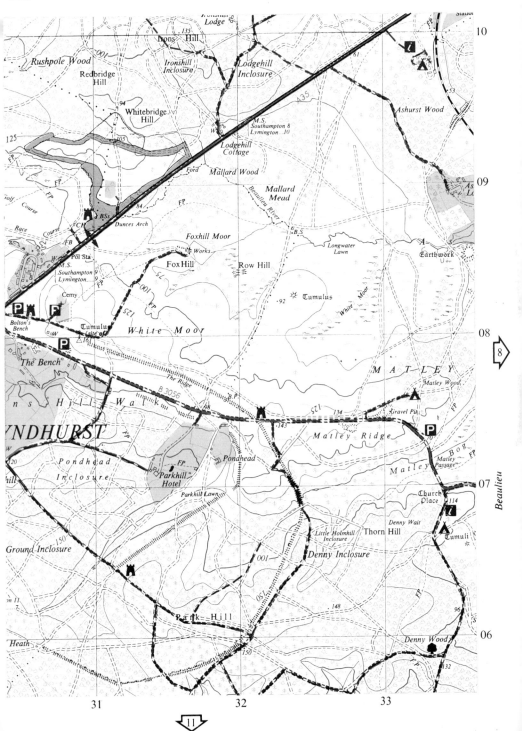

8
ASHURST WALK

This Walk was part of the East Bailiwick, with the Groom Keeper's residence at Ashurst Lodge which is now a private residence. Even today will be found natural regeneration of ash in this walk continuing its long association with its name.

Early resistance to aligning the railway line in 1847 directed it southwards bypassing Lyndhurst and dividing the Walk into east and west halves. Crossing on foot can be made at seven bridges which provide strategic links for walks over the scenic heath, bogland and the Inclosures of Church Place and Deer Leap, the latter deriving its name from a legendary jump by a deer of over eighteen yards which was originally marked by two posts.

At Beaulieu Road Station there is the sale yard where on six occasions during the year New Forest ponies are auctioned to the highest bidder. Ample car park space is available to assist the visitor witness this traditional mart in the Forest.

Provision has been made for a car park in the vicinity of Deer Leap providing access onto open heath walks and into Church Place and Longdown Inclosures. It is also hoped that the small car park adjacent to Yew Tree Heath will afford the walker some walks across this beautiful heathland, specially towards Round-eye Hill. One of the accesses on foot to the Bishop's Dyke may be found from Shatterford car park. A car park is located at Ipley Bridge and is part of the northern Beaulieu River walking complex. Camping is confined to the Ashurst site with access off the A35 just south of Ashurst Village.

1

2

3

1 *Sundew.* [FC]
2 *Petty Whin.* [RF]
3 *Red deer hind.* [TH]
4 *Silver studded blue.* [TH]
5 *Denny Wood camp site.* [DS]
6 *Mallard Wood.* [RF]

4

5

6

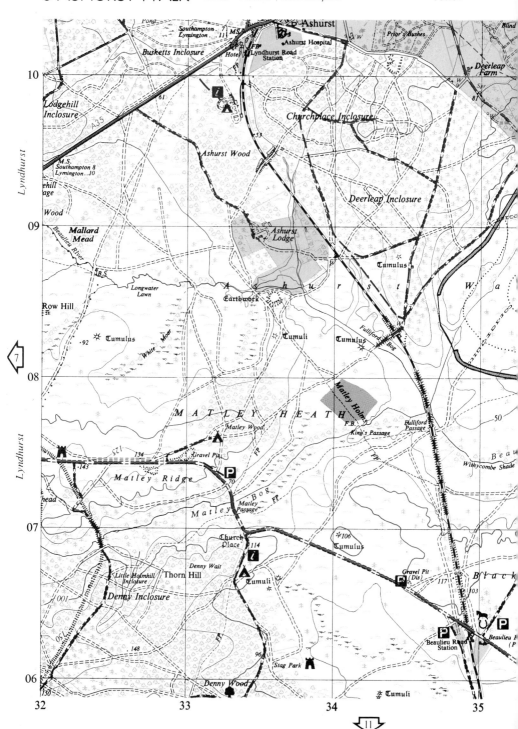

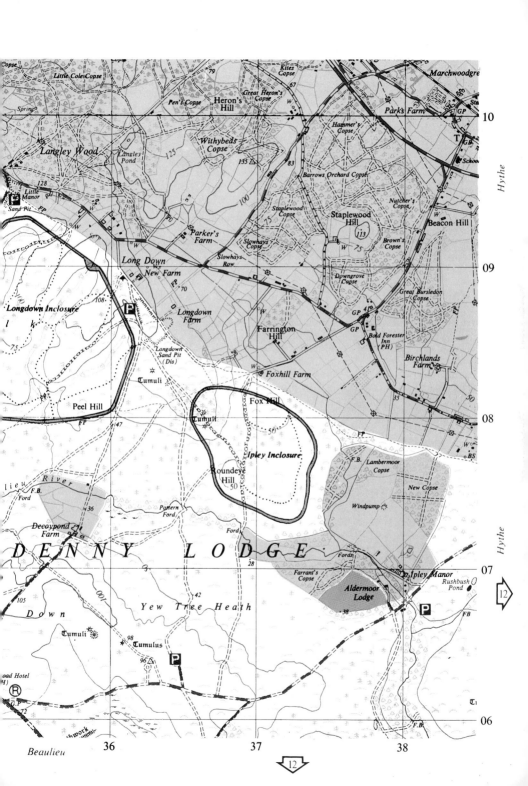

9

BURLEY WALK

Mostly occupied by the Manor of Burley, once the Bailiwick of Burley, under the Dukes of Bolton who between 1680 and 1786 ruled this bailiwick as if it were not Crown property, it is now a large settlement of residences and small holdings, surrounded nevertheless by some of the most contrasting scenery to be found in the Forest.

The western rolling heath and bogland are reminiscent of northern latitudes and in the heath north east of Burley will be found sylvan relics of early fifteenth and sixteenth century encoppicement banks inside which ancient pollarded beech abound. These are ancient relics of the method of feeding deer and supplying fuel wood where the tree in its prime had its head cut off, ie pollard – "to behead" – and the resulting growth of branches was used as coppice supplying fodder and fuelwood. This practice was made illegal in 1698 by William III and today the very heavy branched trees, whose longevity of life is said to be extended by this treatment, are now reaching senility, and, helped by severe winds in the winter, are beginning to disintegrate. In Berry and Ridley Woods are excellent examples for the walker to ponder their true age.

There is an interesting extract from "Book of Survey of Royal Forests" by Roger Taverner, Queen's Surveyor, in 1565 where a reference is made to Ridley Wood where twenty acres of old oak had been topped. This gives an interesting insight as to the possible ages of some of our pollards.

Car parks will be found at Vereley from where an interesting and refreshing walk southwards along Smugglers' Road will remind the walker of another age or northwards along high forest tracks to Ridley Wood across Ridley Green and thence to Berry Wood, where remnants of the pollarding system can be seen, with a return via Turf Croft to Vereley.

Car parks at Undersley Wood and Lucy Hill will lead the walker to interesting Inclosure walks showing a diversity of tree species and the ranges of ages with some fascinating insights to natural wildlife.

For the less energetic, car parks at Burley Lawn, Clay Hill and Burley Cricket Pitch may provide, on certain occasions, a more restful form of entertainment. Concentrations of grazing ponies will often be seen at Spy Holms Lawn, south of which lies an old highway which conveyed the early vehicles from Lymington across the present A35 at Wilverley Post.

1

2

3

1 *Cranes Moor.* [TH]
2 *Sand lizard.* [RF]
3 *Castle Hill from the air.* [SG]
4 *Pollarded beech.* [TH]
5 *Badgers.* [FC]
6 *Stinkhorn fungus.* [HA]

4

5

6

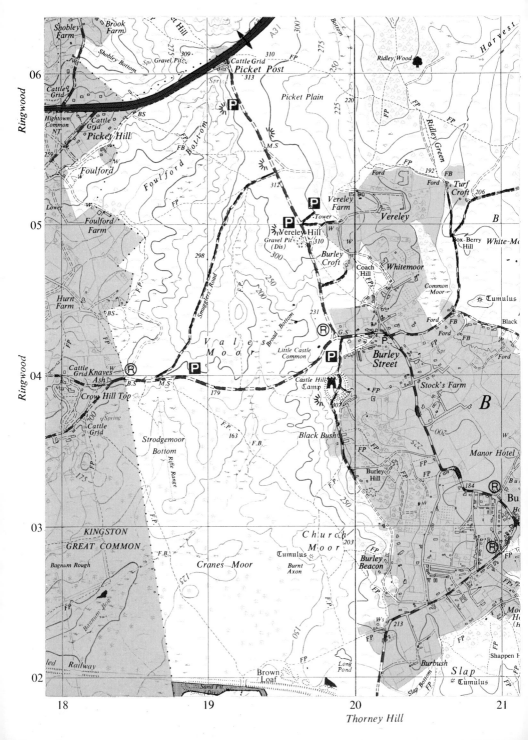

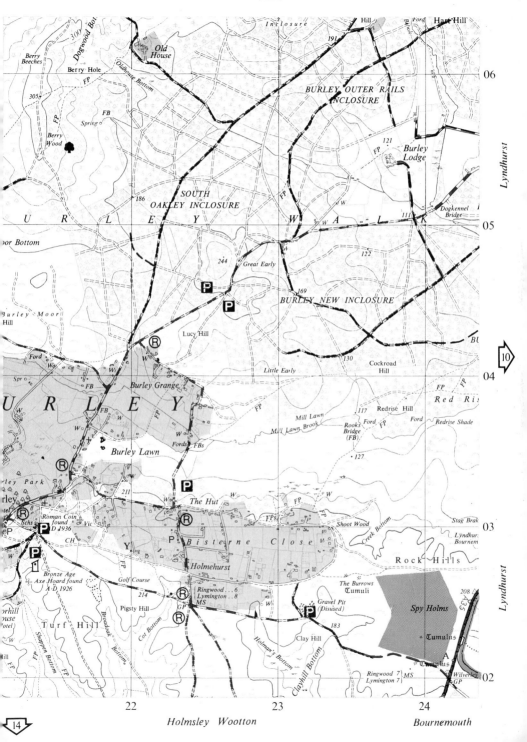

10

RHINEFIELD WALK

The name of this Walk is said to originate from the word "ryge feld" or open land where rye was grown in fields surrounding the present Lodge. This Walk is undoubtedly one of the most popular, lying north west of Brockenhurst. It offers not only open heathland and bogs, but a large tract of enclosed woodland where long and short walks are possible on the network of forest roads and rides.

The Lymington River is swollen by tributaries such as the Ober Water, Black Water and Highland Water, all joining the main river above Balmer Lawn Bridge.

The Groom Keeper's Lodge was said to be originally close to the present Rhinefield House which is now a private residence, built by Lt Munro-Walker after 1877. The name New Park is a distinction from the Old Park at Lyndhurst. The first statutory Inclosure created to grow timber was at Vinney Ridge in 1700 and a small reconstruction of the original bank and pale fence will be seen on the Tall Trees Walk. The favourite walk of Queen Eleanor, wife of Edward I, was said to be to Queen's Bower, which is an area alongside the stream clothed in elderly beech. Markway is alleged to be the site where Hessian troops encamped during the Jacobite Rebellion. It was at Black Knowl that Theodore Roosevelt completed his famous walk in the New Forest from Stoney Cross on 9 June 1910.

The first flying bomb in the 1939–45 war to reach the Forest fell to the west of Puttles Bridge and many incendiary bombs rained down on the forest north of Rhinefield Lodge, causing extensive forest fires.

This Walk is well provided with car parks of all sizes offering special way-marked walks from Blackwater and Brock Hill car parks, where the Tall Trees Walk offers a view of a double avenue of giant conifers. At Puttles Bridge, Aldridge Hill, and Blackwater there is stream-side paddling, picnicking and walking. Whitefield and Whitemoor car parks offer extensive grass lawns on which children can play in safety. Seclusion is also offered at Clumbers with occasional walks into the wilderness to the west.

Extensive exploratory walks into Anderwood and Knightwood Inclosures are available from the Anderwood and Vinney Ridge car parks. From Bolderford Bridge car park charming riverside walks are possible northwards into Highland Water Inclosure.

On the east boundary of this Walk is New Park where equestrian and other recreational activities are organised by arrangement with the Forestry Commission within a 240 acre field system. Camping is available at Aldridge Hill.

1

2

1 *Ober Water, Markway.* [RF]
2 *Tall Trees Walk car park and picnic place.* [RF]
3 *Rhinefield Ornamental Drive.* [TH]
4 *Knightwood oak.* [HA]
5 *Tall Trees forest walk.* [RF]
6 *Recreation at Puttles Bridge.* [RF]

5

4

6

3

FORESTRY COMMISSION
RHINEFIELD
ORNAMENTAL DRIVE
Camping restricted
to camp sites only

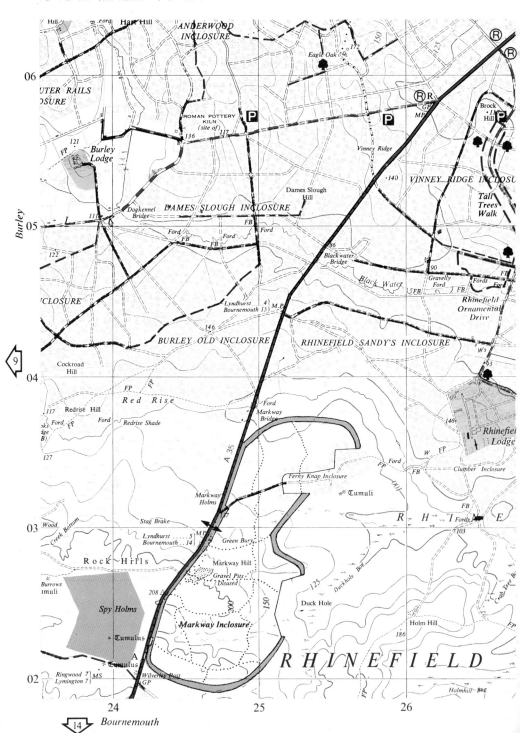

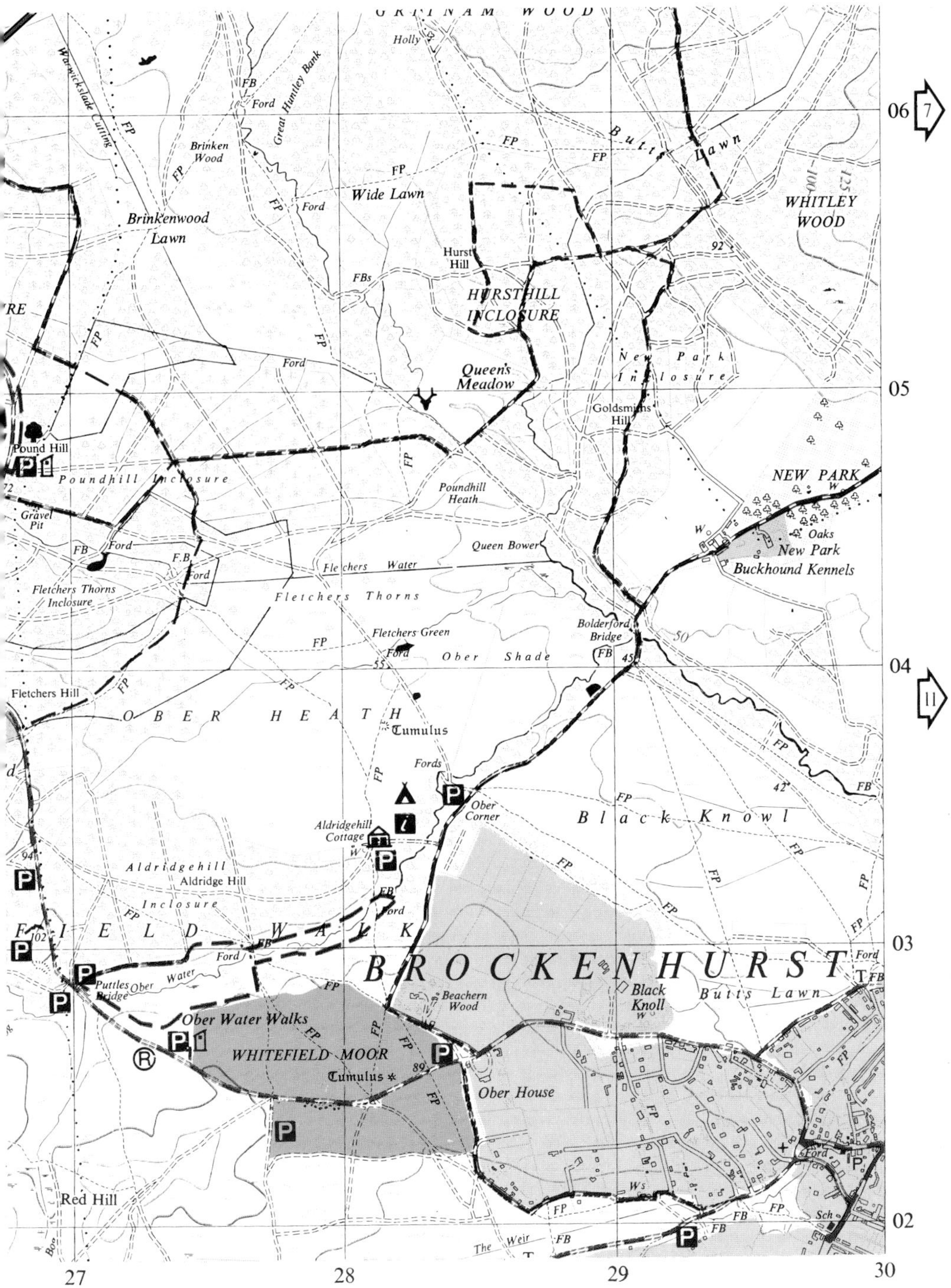

7

GRITNAM WOOD

Holly

FB
Ford

Brinken
Wood

Great Huntley Bank

FP

FP

Butts Lawn

WHITLEY
WOOD

Brinkenwood
Lawn

Wide Lawn

FP

FP

92

125m

Ford

FBs

Hurst
Hill

HURSTHILL
INCLOSURE

RE

FP

Queen's
Meadow

New Park
Inclosure

05

Ford

Pound Hill

Poundhill Inclosure

FP

Goldsmiths
Hill

NEW PARK

Gravel
Pit

2

Poundhill
Heath

Queen Bower

W

Oaks
New Park
Buckhound Kennels

FB Ford

F.B.
ord

Fletchers Water

Queen Bower

W

Fletchers Thorns
Inclosure

Fletchers Thorns

Fletchers Green

Bolderford
Bridge

50

04

Fletchers Hill

FP

FP

Ford

Ober Shade

55

FB 45

OBER HEATH

Tumulus

Black Knowl

42

FB

d

FP

Fords

FP

Aldridgehill
Cottage

Ober
Corner

FP

W

Aldridgehill
Inclosure

Aldridge Hill

94

FB

FIELD WALK

Ford

FB

BROCKENHURST

Ford

T FB

P

F

02

Puttles
Bridge

Ober Water

Ford

Beachern
Wood

Black
Knoll

Butts Lawn

R

Ober Water Walks

WHITEFIELD MOOR

Tumulus

89

Ober House

FP

P

Red Hill

Ws

Sch

02

FP

FB

The Weir

FB

27 28 29 30

15

11

WHITLEY RIDGE WALK

This Walk originally went southwards to include the now privately-owned Brockenhurst Park and for convenience in the presentation in this Guide it now takes in part of the westerly Denny Lodge Walk. It embraces one of the largest continuous tracts of woodland in the Forest, severed only by the main railway line. Balmer Lawn is a large forest lawn kept well grazed by ponies and cattle, a one-time race course for New Forest ponies, and is now surrounded by self regenerating woodlands such as Hollands and Whitley Woods and in the north east by a unique area of bog surrounded by a medieval earthwork said to have been the boundary of church land resulting from a famous crawl by the Bishop of Winchester. On the east lies Frame Wood, which is a fine example of woodland regenerating naturally since 1860 in spite of intense grazing both by ponies and deer.

An historic link with the past will be found on the track leading through Hollands Wood camp site northwards to Ashurst – an ancient saltway where the salt obtained from the salterns on the coast was transported from Lymington to Ashurst.

During the assembly of troops for the invasion of France in the 1939–45 war, Balmer Lawn Hotel was used by the US air force during the run-up to D-Day, and the cricket pavilion served as a post office for American forces awaiting the invasion of Europe.

The Inclosures are numerous and are well linked by gravel forest roads essential for strategic management and emergencies but made available for pedestrian use. Extensive walks are possible linked from the few car parks north and south of the railway line. South of this railway line will be found the main home of the Japanese Sika deer and on the north side will be found Roe and Fallow, which will often be seen on the grass rides in the early or late part of the day.

Car parks are situated at Balmer Lawn riverside, Standing Hat, Ivy Wood, Ladycross, Stockley and Hawkhill.

Camping is available at Hollands Wood and Roundhill, with emergency overflow areas at Beaulieu Heath.

1 *Broad bodied chaser.* [TH]
2 *Cotton grass.* [RF]
3 *Hollands Wood open forest.* [HA]
4 *Bog myrtle.* [HA]
5 *Hollands Wood campsite.* [RF]
6 *Sika stag with hinds.* [RF]
7 *Forest donkeys.* [RF]

3
4

6
7

5

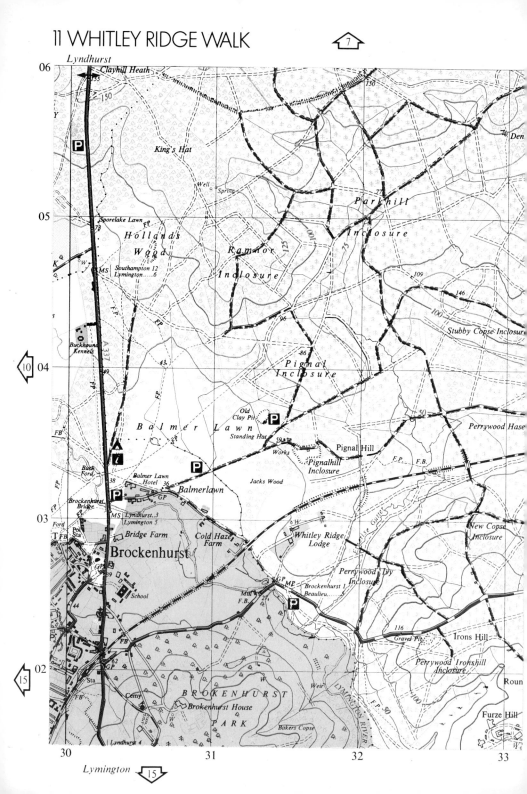

Lyndhurst

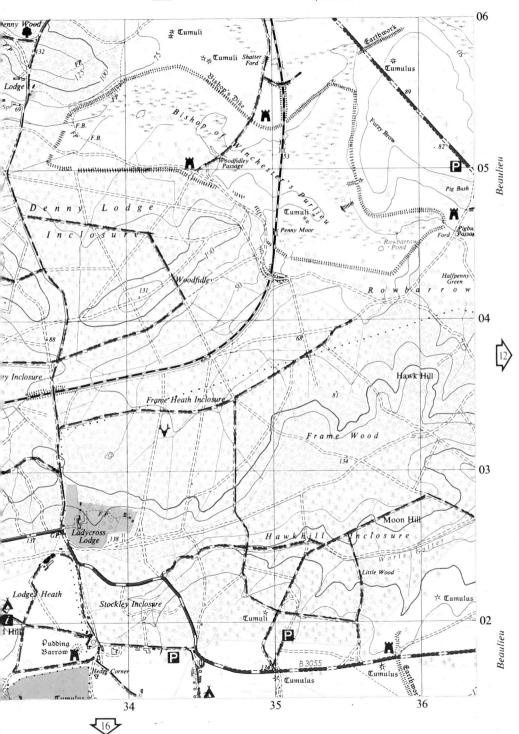

Beaulieu

Beaulieu

12 & 13
DENNY LODGE WALK

This Walk embraces the largest parish by area in the United Kingdom, with a total population of 470 in 1973, and is depicted on two maps with parts still included in the Ashurst Walk. It extends from Matley Heath (Ashurst) to King's Copse Inclosure near Fawley in the south. The original Groom Keeper's Lodge is situated in the centre and is now a Head Forester's residence.

It is chiefly heath and bogland, with new Inclosures planted on the eastern boundary between 1963 and 1965 in an attempt to screen the waterside industrial landscape. These Inclosures are growing well and will one day offer the visitor a welcome respite from the industrial scenery. The well-wooded and efficiently farmed Beaulieu Estate abuts on to the southern boundary of this Walk and offers the visitor to the Forest a variety of interests including the National Motor Museum.

There is an abundance of ancient bronze age burial barrows scattered over the heathland but tragically all have been destroyed by early incompetent excavations.

There are few remnants of Roman occupation in the Forest other than occasional pottery kilns in the north; however, a Roman Road with a prominent agger (camber) can still be seen in Fawley Inclosure.

Car parks at Culverley offer walks westwards into the delightful Tantany, Stubbs and Hawkhill Ancient and Ornamental Woodlands of great maturity. Access is also possible from this car park, for those who are careful to Bishop's Dyke earthworks. Car parks at North Gate, King's Hat, and Ipley Bridge make available to the walker the Beaulieu riverside and the fine open lawns of Brick Hill.

King's Copse Inclosure is the most easterly island of woodland in the Forest and offers the walker short walks on the forest ride system, possibly unaware of how close are the Refinery and Power Station of Fawley.

In complete contrast a lakeside car park will be found at Hatchet Pond, overlooking this artificial pond where bird life abounds. A narrow causeway path has been constructed to enable the walker safely to proceed southwards without having to regain access on to the highway.

1

2

3

1 *Redshank.* [TH]
2 *Kings Copse Inclosure.* [DS]
3 *Orange peel peziza.* [RF]
4 *Bog pimpernel.* [HA]
5 *Culverley car park and picnic place.* [RF]
6 *Sphagnum bog, Bishop's Dyke.* [HA]

5

4

6

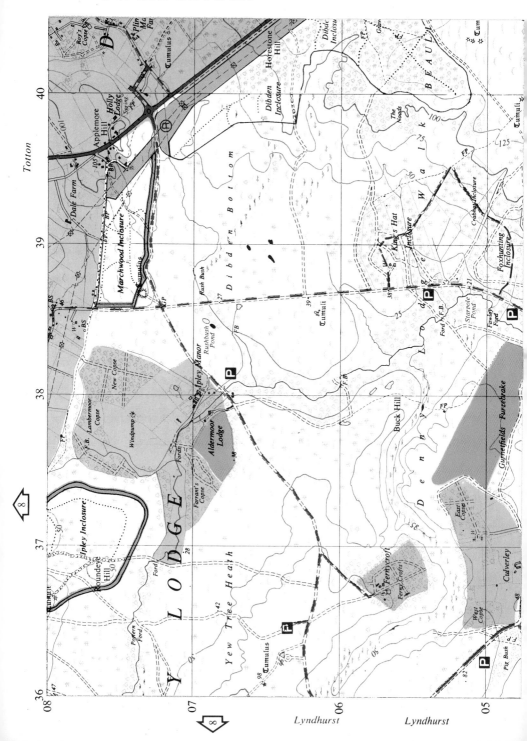

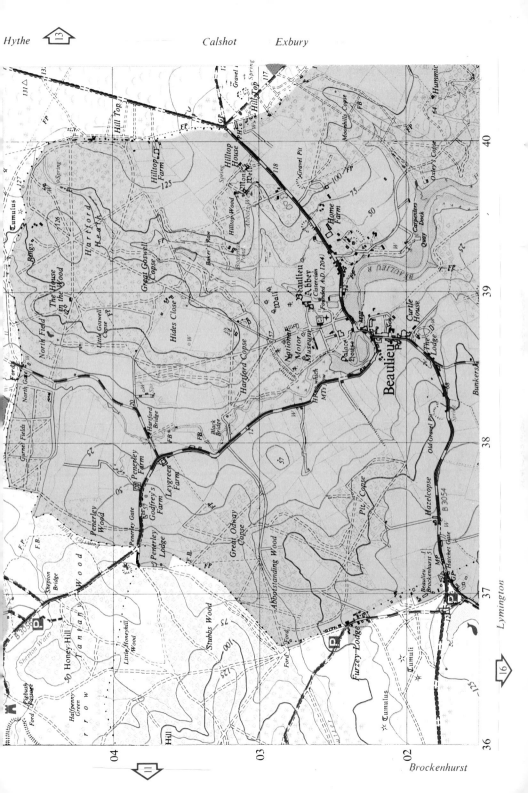

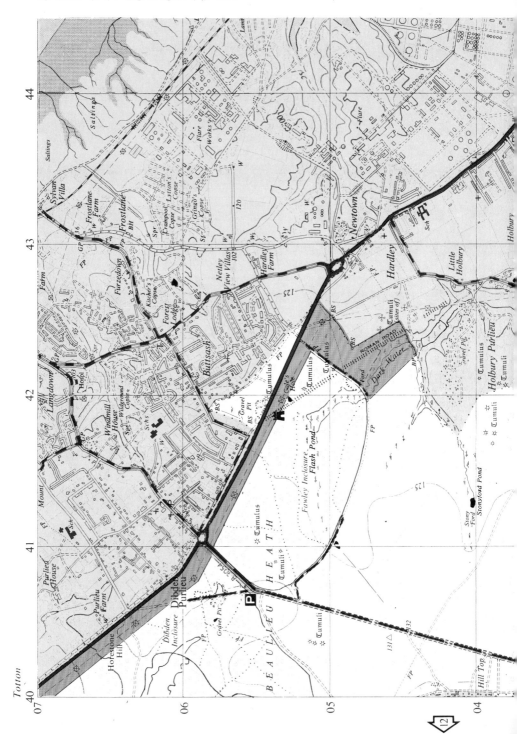

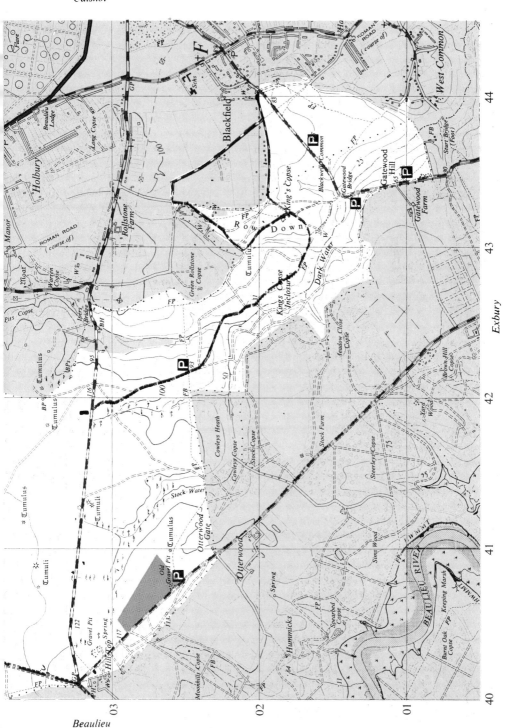

14

HOLMSLEY WALK

Deriving its name from "holm" (holly), extensive copses called "Hats" existed prior to the construction of the airfield in 1942. Relics of these can still be seen to the north of the camp site, as it exists today, with such delightful names as Great Hat, Bell's Hat and Thorney Hill Holms. The Groom Keeper's Lodge is today a private residence. Records show that this airfield, opened in September 1942, was used extensively by many different types of aircraft and latterly made a major contribution to the invasion of Europe in 1944. It was closed in 1946. In May 1940 the first German high explosive bomb fell at Wilverley Post, killing a pony.

This Walk is comparatively speaking a small one but still offers some scenic gems to the adventurous walker as he traverses the great expanse of natural heath at Dur Hill Down overlooking Bisterne Common and Whitten Bottom. The Inclosures are well served by streams and are rich with insect life. Holmsley, Brownhill and Wootton Coppice are worthy of exploring with their neat small plantations of all ages and species.

Car parks are available at Dur Hill, Burbush, Holmsley Ridge, Goatspen, Ossemsley Ford, Wilverley Post and Pigsty Hill, each offering a change of scenery and walks of varied length and interest.

Camping is confined to the Holmsley Airfield and the woodlands behind, where modern facilities will be found.

1

2

4

1 *Roe kid*. [RF]
2 *Dur Hill heath*. [RF]
3 *Silver-washed fritillary*. [RF]
4 *Bog asphodel*. [HA]
5 *Holmsley camp site*. [RF]
6 *Beech stump "garden"*. [RF]

3

5

6

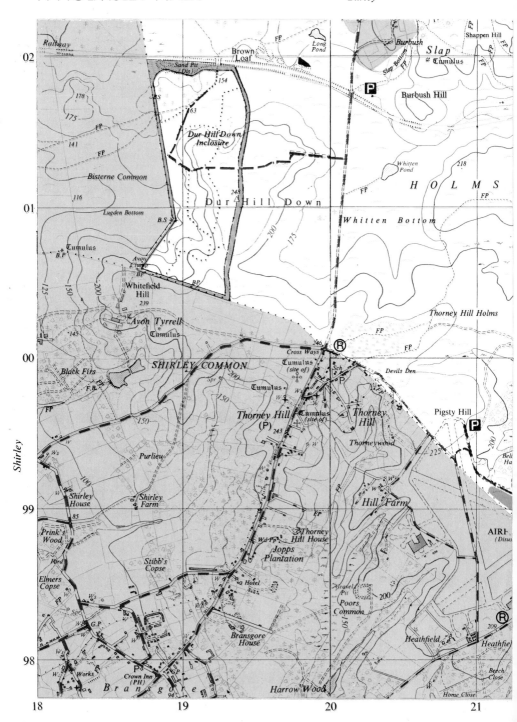

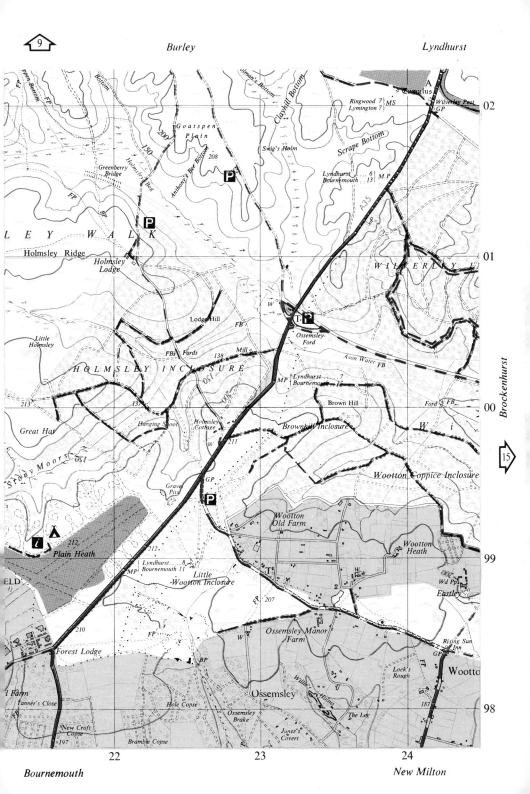

15
WILVERLEY WALK

Believed to be named after the natural willows of the Avon Water which traverses this southern part on its way eastwards to the sea, this Walk offers a wide variety of open heath, artificially reseeded lawns, mature Inclosures, fascinating bogs and associated natural lawns. There are some fine views of Rhinefield Walk, particularly from Hincheslea Plain in the late evening, when a panoramic landscape can be viewed with the sun in the west. Grazing ponies and cattle are often concentrated at Wilverley Plain and Longslade Bottom.

The names of Inclosures and woodland, if studied with the assistance of the Oxford Dictionary of English Place Names by Ekwall, will often confirm how the original tree crops were established. For example, Setthorns owes its name to acorns being sown with thorn as hawes, to aid their survival against grazing.

The "Naked Man" is a relic of a gibbet tree referred to in Chapter 7.

Car parks afford a wide variety of peaceful pastimes, notably at Wootton Bridge, Broadley, Boundway Hill, Setthorns, Longslade Bottom, Horseshoe Bottom, Wilverley Plain, Wilverley Pit, Hincheslea Viewpoint, Hincheslea Moor, Hincheslea Bog and Setley Pond.

Camping is confined to within Setthorns Inclosure where gravel pitches for caravans are separated by trees and undergrowth.

The main London–Bournemouth railway passes through the southern section of this Walk, stopping at Sway and Brockenhurst.

1 *Bastard balm.* [RF]
2 *Pine male flowers.* [HA]
3 *Wootton Bridge car park at Avon Water.* [RF]
4 *Longslade Bottom.* [HA]
5 *Stag beetle.* [RF]
6 *Larch female flowers.* [HA]
7 *Wilverley Inclosure from the air, 1971.* [FC]
8 *Wilverley Plain from the air, 1971.* [FC]

3

4

5

6

7

8

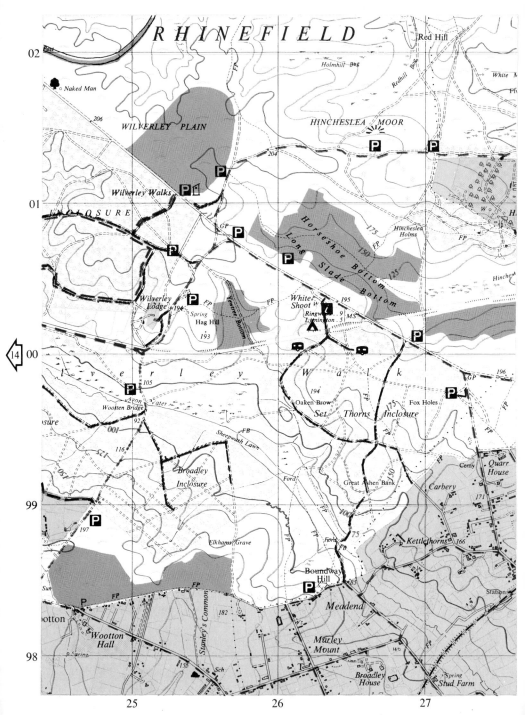

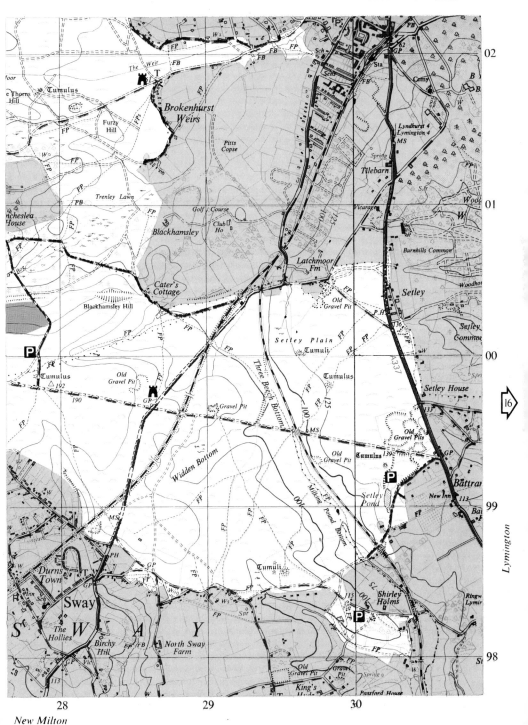

02

01

00

99

98

The Weir
Brokenhurst Weirs
Pitts Copse
Trenley Lawn
Golf Course
Blackhamsley
Club Ho
Cater's Cottage
Blackhamsley Hill
Setley Plain
Tumuli
Tumulus
Old Gravel Pit
Three Beech Bottom
Gravel Pit
Widden Bottom
Tumulus
Old Gravel Pit
Milking Pound Bottom
Setley Pond
New Inn
Tumuli
Shirley Holms
Durns Town
Sway
The Hollies
Birchy Hill
North Sway Farm
King's

Sch
Sta
Cemy
Lyndhurst 4
Lymington 4
MS
Tilebarn
Vicarage
Latchmoor Fm
Setley
Burnhills Common
Woodhou
Setley Common
Setley House
Old Gravel Pits
Battra
Setley Plain
Woo
W

New Milton

28   29   30

Lymington

16

16
LADY CROSS WALK

This Walk is fairly flat with magnificent skyscapes to be seen in changeable weather. The Isle of Wight can be seen from the open places made more exposed by the construction of Beaulieu Airfield in 1942, from where in 1944 major attacks on flying bombs and invasion targets were made. The use of this airfield continued right up until November 1959. Some of the old runways have been removed but the remainder are being maintained to afford the visitor a complete contrast to the enclosed landscapes of the central walks. One of the major attractions is Hatchet Pond which has been stocked with coarse fish offering fishing on permits from the Forestry Commission. It is believed it was originally the water storage supply for a mill in East Boldre.

There are many Bronze Age barrows throughout this area, alas no longer retaining their original profile. In the south is the only Inclosure to be found, Norley, which is a southern outlier offering sheltered walks amidst the plantations of tomorrow.

Car parks are available at Beaulieu Old Airfield; Hatchet Moor; Crockford; Crockford Clump – where the early field system can be seen on the ground as referred to in Chapter 2, Bull Hill and Norley, each offering a contrast and in some cases shelter from whichever way the wind blows.

The numerous rectangular water-filled hollows alongside the road from Lymington to Beaulieu have naturally evolved into miniature pond habitats. They owe their origin to the anti-aircraft gun positions used in the Second World War to defend Beaulieu airfield.

1

2

3

4

1 *Crossleaved heather.* [RF]
2 *Purple heather.* [HA]
3 *Ling.* [HA]
4 *Beaulieu Heath with the Isle of Wight in the distance from the air, 1971.* [FC]
5 *Hatchet Pond.* [HA]
6 *Hatchet Pond car park.* [FC]
7 *Crockford Clump car park.* [RF]

5

6

7

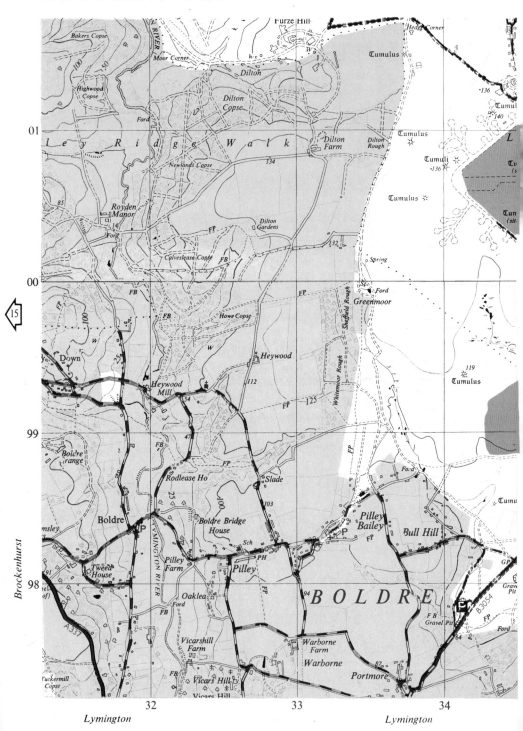

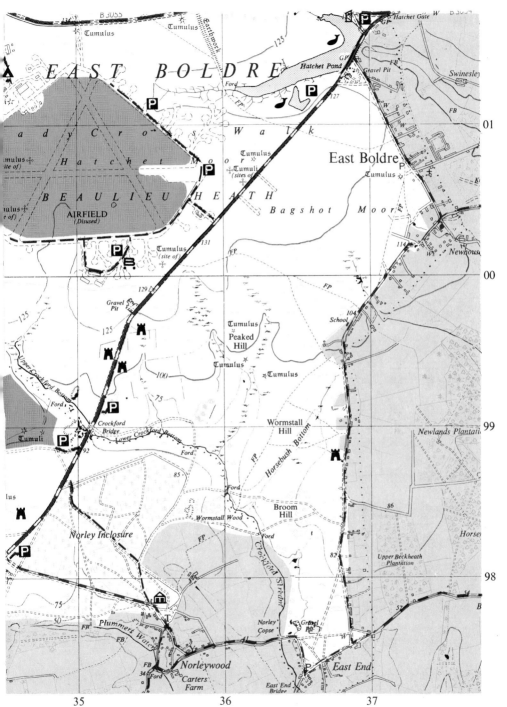

Fifteen

General information

How to reach the Forest

By train: the main station and motorail terminal for the Forest is Brockenhurst, and most Waterloo–Bournemouth trains stop there. Local trains stop at Lyndhurst Road, Beaulieu Road and Sway. Southampton and Bournemouth are the nearest major stations. British Rail enquiries: Southampton 229393.

By coach: National Express Services from London (Victoria Coach Station, SW1).

By bus: local services are operated by Hants & Dorset Motor Services Ltd, Arndale Centre, Poole (673555).

By road: via M3 (London), M27 (south-east coast), A34 (north and midlands). Overnight parking in the Forest (except as permitted for camping) is against the Byelaws.

By air: Hurn Airport, Bournemouth.

By ferry: from Southampton across the Solent to Hythe (pedestrians and cyclists only). Car ferries to Lymington from the Isle of Wight.

Camping

The Forestry Commission's camp sites are open from the Friday before Good Friday each year until the end of September. Ashurst camp stays open until the end of October and Setthorns remains open all the year round. Full details from the Forestry Commission, The Queen's house, Lyndhurst (042 128 3771). It is an offence under the Byelaws to camp without a permit or elsewhere than on an official site.

Holiday accommodation

The Forest is well supplied with hotels, the majority being in Lyndhurst and Brockenhurst: list from New Forest District Council, Appletree Court, Lyndhurst, Hants SO4 7PA (042 128 3121). There are Youth Hostels in the area, details of which may be had from the Youth Hostels Association, 8 St Stephen's Hill, St Albans, Herts. (0727 55215).

Riding and Sports

There are many riding schools and livery stables in and around the Forest, see address

1 *Camping.* [HI]
2 *Riding.* [RF]
3 *Fishing.* [HI]

below. The district has its own packs of fox-hounds, buckhounds and beagles.

Permits for fishing (coarse and trout) may be had from the Queen's House, Lyndhurst, or from camping offices during the season.

There are golf courses at Lyndhurst, Burley, Brockenhurst and Bramshaw.

Wildlife conservation

All wild life in the Forest is protected by the Byelaws. Permission to study or collect specimens for scientific purposes must be sought in writing from the Deputy Surveyor.

Useful local addresses

Clerk to the Verderers, The Queen's House, Lyndhurst (2052).

New Forest District Council, Appletree Court, Lyndhurst (3121)

Hampshire Constabulary, The Police Station, Lydnhurst (2813)

New Forest Association – Hon Secretary Mrs L K Errington, Rockford End, Ringwood, Hampshire.

New Forest Pony Breeding and Cattle Society – Hon Secretary Miss D M Macnair, Beacon Corner, Burley, Ringwood, Hampshire

Hampshire Field Club (New Forest Section) – Hon Secretary Mrs J Irvine, 4 Clarence Road, Lyndhurst, Hampshire.

Association of New Forest Riding Establishments – Chairman Mr D A Horton, Decoy Pond Farm, Beaulieu Road, Brockenhurst, Hampshire.

Nature Conservancy Council, 1 Southampton Road, Lyndhurst (3944).

Hampshire County Council, The Castle, Winchester (54411).

Tourist Information Centre, Lyndhurst (2269).

Land area

Distribution of Land Ownership within the Perambulation

Figures show total area in hectares. 1 hectare=2.47 acres

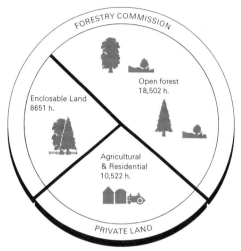

FORESTRY COMMISSION

Open forest
18,502 h.

Enclosable Land
8651 h.

Agricultural
& Residential
10,522 h.

PRIVATE LAND

Total Area 37,675 h. (93,082 acres)

Distribution of Vegetation within Forestry Commission Areas

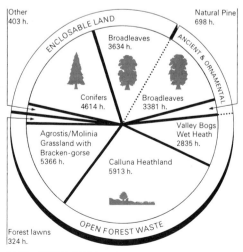

Other
403 h.

Natural Pine
698 h.

ENCLOSABLE LAND

Broadleaves
3634 h.

ANCIENT & ORNAMENTAL

Conifers
4614 h.

Broadleaves
3381 h.

Valley Bogs
Wet Heath
2835 h.

Agrostis/Molinia
Grassland with
Bracken-gorse
5366 h.

Calluna Heathland
5913 h.

Forest lawns
324 h.

OPEN FOREST WASTE

Total Area 27,157 h. (67,082 acres)

1

1 *Brockenhurst Church.* [RF]
2 *Roe Cottage and Inclosure.* [RF]

A note on books

The most valuable modern scientific work is *The New Forest: An Ecological Study* by Colin R Tubbs, published in 1969. Well illustrated, it embraces all aspects of field natural history and agricultural economy. Anthony Pasmore's *Verderers of the New Forest*, published in 1977, gives a historical account of the Forest since 1877.

The classic work on the New Forest is that entitled *The New Forest, its History and Scenery*, by John R Wise (Gibbings, London) first published in 1863. Although long out of print, it ran through several editions and second-hand copies are fairly easy to find. The main text deals with the history, topography, scenery and customs of the Forest, whilst the appendices include lists of plants, birds and insects, and an interesting glossary of the local dialect.

There are many more recent works that describe and illustrate the Forest's attractions in a more popular style, including the following:
The New Forest by De Crespigny & Hutchinson, 1895
The New Forest by Mrs Rawnsley, 1904
The New Forest by Horace Hutchinson, 1904
The New Forest by E Godfrey, 1912
Hampshire's Glorious Wilderness by G R Tweedie, 1925
The New Forest Beautiful by F E Stevens, 1925
Walking in the New Forest by Joan Begbie, 1934
The New Forest by John C Moore, 1934
The New Forest published by Messrs Dent, 1960

Remarks on Forest Scenery (2 vols, 1791) is a well-known work by the Rev William Gilpin, sometime Vicar of Boldre, who had much to say on the beauties of trees in the Forest landscape. An interesting record of sporting life in the Forest is to be found in *Thirty-five Years in the New Forest* (1915) by the Hon Gerald Lascelles, a former Deputy Surveyor. The great authority on the Forest's archaeology was Heywood Sumner, whose published works include:

Ancient Earthworks of the New Forest, 1917, *A Map of Ancient Sites in the New Forest*, 1923, *Guide to the New Forest*, 1924, *Excavations in New Forest Roman Pottery Sites*, 1927, *Local Papers, Archaeological and Topographical, Hants, Dorset and Wilts*, 1931.

Dr F E Kenchington has described the history and customs of the Commoners, and the war-time schemes for the improvement of the Forest grazing, very fully in *The Commoners New Forest* (Hutchinson, London, 1943). Very full accounts of the Forest's history and topography appear in the *Victoria County History of Hampshire* (1900, 6 vols), which includes an informative article on forestry by Lascelles and Nisbet.

The best known work of fiction having a New Forest background is probably *The Children of the New Forest* (1853) by F Marryatt, a story of Civil War days. R D Blackmore was the author of *Cradock Nowell; a Tale of the New Forest*, a three-volume work published in 1866. Mrs Gaskell featured the New Forest in her *North and South*, 1855, as did Conan Doyle in his *The White Company*, 1891. Children of all ages will enjoy two more modern and well-illustrated stories by Allen W Seaby, entitled *Skewbald, the New Forest Pony*, and *The White Hart*, the latter story being based on the life of a white deer which actually roamed the Rhinefield woods a few years ago.

There is a wealth of modern guides to the forest obtainable from local bookshops: in Lyndhurst A L Margerison, 40 High Street (2270), also King's of Lymington (72137) and the Ringwood Bookshop (4802).

The Killing of William Rufus, by Duncan Grinnell-Milne (David & Charles, Newton Abbot, 1968) is a thrilling investigation into the Forest's best-known historical event.

Wilverley Plain and Inclosure with Spy Holms in the background from the air, 1971, looking north-west [FC], *and the Ordnance Survey map of the same area.*

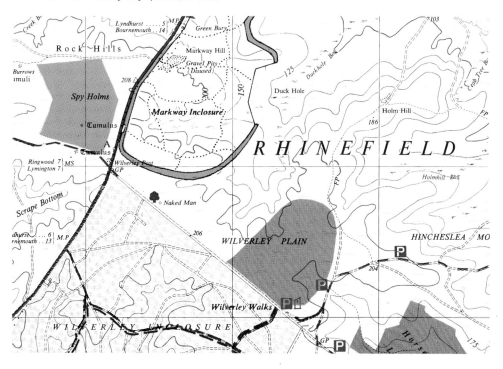

Legend to the maps

	M 4 *or* A 6(M) A 123 *or* A 123(T)

Motorway. *Trunk and Main Road (Dual Carriageway)*

Trunk & Main Road .... A 123 *or* A 123(T)

Secondary Road .... Fenced   B 2314   Unfenced

Road Under Construction ....

Other Roads .... Good, metalled   Poor, or unmetalled

Footpaths .... FP   FP
       Fenced   Unfenced

Railways, Multiple Track .... Station   Road over   FB
      Sidings   Cutting   Tunnel   (*Footbridge*)

,,   *Single Track* .,,   Viaduct   Level Crossing   Embankment   Road under

,,   *Narrow Gauge*

Aerial Ropeway .... Aerial Ropeway

Boundaries { *County or County Borough* ....
          ,, ,, County of City (in Scotland)

,,   ,, ,, ,, ,, ,, with Parish ....

,,   Parish ....

Pipe Line (Oil, Water) .... Pipe Line

Electricity Transmission Lines (Pylons shown at bends and spaced conventionally) –

Post Offices (In Villages & Rural Areas only) .... P   *Town Hall* ....TH   *Public House* ...... PH

Church or Chapel with Tower   *Church or Chapel with Spire*   *Church or Chapel without either*

Triangulation Station .... △   *on Church with Tower* ....   *without Tower* ....

Intersected Point on Chy ....○   *on Church with Spire* ....   *without Spire* .....   *on Building* ....

Guide Post   GP.   *Mile Post* ....MP.   *Mile Stone* ...MS.   *Boundary Stone* ...BS ○   *Boundary Post* ...BP○

Youth Hostel   Y   *Telephone Call Box (Public)*   T   *(AA)* A   *(RAC)* R   *Antiquity (site of)*

Public Buildings	*Glasshouses*	
Quarry & Gravel Pit	*Orchard*	
National Trust Area .... (Sheen Common NT)	*Furze*	
,, ,, ,, Scotland ......NTS	*Rough Pasture Heath & Moor*	
Osier Bed	*Marsh*	
Reeds	*Well* .... W ○	
Park, Fenced	*Spring* .... Spr ○	
Wood, Coniferous, Fenced	*Wind Pump* .... Wd Pp .	
Wood, Non-Coniferous Unfenced	The grid lines on this sheet are at 1 kilometre interval.	
Brushwood, Fenced & Unfenced	Contours are at 25 feet vertical interval.	
	Spot Height ....123·	

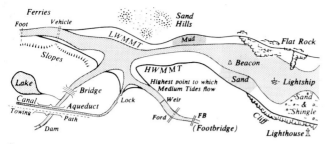

Ferries
Foot Vehicle
Sand Hills
L W M M T
Mud
Flat Rock
Slopes
△ Beacon
H W M M T
Highest point to which Medium Tides flow
Sand
Lightship
Lake
Bridge
Lock
Weir
Sand
Canal
Aqueduct
Towing Path
Ford
FB
(Footbridge)
Dam
Cliff
Sand & Shingle
Lighthouse ⚓

© Crown copyright 1975

FOOTPATHS (NEW FOREST CROWN LAND ONLY)
The representation of any road, track or path is no evidence of the existence of a public right of way. There are no public rights of way over the New Forest (other than the metalled surface of any highway maintained by the Highway authority) but the public are permitted to use existing paths on foot for air and exercise.

Forestry Commission tourist information added to Ordnance Survey maps.

The reproduction of a boundary is approximate and is not intended to depict the limits of land title.

Private land

Forest Information

Forest car parks and picnic places

Forest viewpoints

Forest toilets

Forest barbecue sites reserved by application to Queen's House

Forestry Commission camp sites: tents and caravans

Forestry Commission camp sites: caravans only

Private camp sites: tents and caravans

Forest access road, official vehicle access only except for access to car parks and camp sites

Forest underpass, horse-drawn vehicles, animals and pedestrians only

Width restriction on County roads not exceeding 6' 6"

Forest waymarked walks

Forest lawns or grazing strips

Wildlife Centres

Deer observation towers reserved by application to Queen's House

Forest fishing by permit only

Ornamental and historic trees

Selected historic locations

Pony sales

Acknowledgements and contributors

DESIGN HMSO/Dennis Greeno.

GRAPHIC ILLUSTRATION Gary Hincks.

PHOTOGRAPHS Heather Angel, F.R.P.S., Robin Fletcher, Vision International, Hugh Insley, Norman Orr, A.R.P.S., Donn Small, OBE., Forestry Commission photographic staff, led by I A Anderson, F.I.I.P., Richard Prior, Terry Heathcote, Colin Palmer, Tony Russell, Geoff Green and Southern Gas.

SOURCE MATERIAL FOR ILLUSTRATION The British Museum and the Hampshire Record Office, Winchester.

MAPS The Ordnance Survey, by kind permission of the Controller of Her Majesty's Stationery Office.

MRS K MERLE CHACKSFIELD a former Hampshire Headmistress, has made a special study of smuggling, and is the author of a popular book, "Smuggling Days" (Dorset Publishing Co.). She has lectured and written numerous articles on the subject. She is also an artist. Amongst her other works are books on modern educational methods. Her latest publication is "The Dorset and Somerset Rebellion" (D.P.C. 1985), an account of the Monmouth Rebellion of 1685.

JOHN CHAPMAN is on the staff of the Forestry Commission at Lyndhurst.

MICHAEL CLARKE is a Head Keeper of the New Forest; he has an enthusiastic and practical knowledge of deer management and is a knowledgeable naturalist.

DAVID COBB is a professional marine artist who lives locally and has made a special study of the architectural history of the wooden ship.

MALDWIN DRUMMOND is an elected Verderer of the New Forest and a Countryside Commissioner. He went to the Royal Agricultural College, Cirencester before taking up farming and forestry on the south eastern fringe of the Forest, on the Solent shore. He is a Justice of the Peace for Hampshire and holds a Certificate in Environmental Science from Southampton University.

HUGH INSLEY was a professional Forest Officer on the staff of the Deputy Surveyor. He is an enthusiastic and knowledgeable naturalist.

ARTHUR T LLOYD is a retired history teacher, who has made a study in depth of derivations of local names and is renowned for his new contributions to the interpretation of historical records.

MISS DIONIS MACNAIR was born at Burley in the New Forest. She has had ponies in the Forest since she was a child and teaches all branches of riding. She is an elected Verderer, a member of the Council of the Commoners' Defence Association and has been Honorary Secretary of the New Forest Pony Breeding and Cattle Society since 1967.

ANTHONY PASMORE is an elected Verderer, Vice Chairman of the New Forest Section of the Hampshire Field Club, a member of the Councils of the Commoners' Defence Association and the New Forest Association, and of the Hale Purlieu Advisory Committee. He is an amateur local historian and archaeologist, and a Chartered Surveyor.

HUGH C PASMORE came to live at Fritham in the New Forest in 1933 and apart from war service has remained in the Forest ever since. He practised as a Chartered Surveyor until 1965. For the past thirty years he has bred New Forest ponies. He was appointed a Verderer by the Minister of Agriculture in 1968 but has now retired. He is a member of the Council of the New Forest Association and for many years contributed to local newspapers a monthly article entitled "A New Forest Commoner's Notebook".

DONN SMALL served as Deputy Surveyor of the New Forest from 1971 to 1983, being responsible for a far-reaching programme of conservation measures for which he was awarded the OBE. Previously he was in the Colonial Forest Service in Sierra Leone and with the Forestry Commission in East Anglia and the Chilterns.

BERRY STONE map revision for third impression.

MRS MARJORIE TRIGGS has lived in or near the Forest all her life. She is an experienced researcher into ancient documents and records.

DAVID J STAGG is a local historian and archaeologist, and takes an active part in Forest affairs.

COLIN TUBBS is Senior County Officer for the Nature Conservancy Council for Hampshire and the Isle of Wight, a naturalist and expert on the ecology of the New Forest.

Index

Index to place names, within crown property as printed on Ordnance Survey Maps 1:25000 scale in this guide.

To locate name two references are given.
a. First figure refers to map number.
b. Second four figures locate the lower left hand grid reference of the kilometre square eg 2016.

Blackensford Bottom 6/2207
Blackensford Hill 6/2307
Blackensford Lawn 6/2306
Blackfield 13/4302
Black Gutter 1/2016
Black Gutter Bottom 1/2016
Blackhamsley Hill 15/2800
Black Heath 5/1810
Black Hill 9/2104
Black Knowl 10/2903
Black Water 10/2504
Blackwater Bridge 10/2504
Blackwell Common 13/4301
Blissford Hill 1/1713
Bolderford Bridge 10/2804
Bolderwood Cottage 6/2408
Bolderwood Farm 6/2308
Bolderwood Green 6/2408
Bolderwood Grounds 6/2308
Bolderwood Hill 6/2408
Bolderwood Walks 6/2408
Bolton's Bench 7/3008
Boundway Hill 15/2698
Box Berry Hill 9/2004
Bramble Hill 2/2515
Bramble Hill 7/2706
Bramshaw 2/2615
Bramshaw Hill 3/2614
Bramshaw Incl 2/2516
Bramshaw Telegraph 2/2216
Bramshaw Wood 2/2516
Bratley Arch 6/2309
Bratley Incl 5/2208
Bratley Water 6/2310
Bratley Wood 5/2208
Brick Kiln Incl 7/2906
Brinkenwood Lawn 10/2705
Brinkenwood 10/2705
Broad Bottom 9/1904
Broadley Incl 15/2599
Broadoak Bottom 9/2102
Broadway Bottom 3/2213
Brockenhurst 11/3002
Brockenhurst Weirs 15/2801
Brock Hill 10/2605
Brockis Hill 4/2911
Brockis Hill Incl 7/7011
Brogenslade Bottom 5/1811
Brook Common 3/2613
Brook Hill 3/2614
Broom Hill 3/2614
Broom Hill 16/3698
Broom Hill 6/2708
Broomy Bottom 3/2111
Broomy Incl 5/2011
Broomy Lodge 5/2011
Broomy Plain 5/2010
Brown Hill 14/2300
Brownhill Incl 14/2399
Brown Loaf 14/1902
Buckherd Bottom 5/2008
Buck Ford 11/3003
Buck Hill 12/3705
Bull Hill 16/3398
Bunkers Hill 7/2909
Burbush 9/2002
Bur Bushes 2/2116
Burbush Hill 14/2001
Burley 9/2103

Burley Beacon 9/2202
Burley Croft 9/1904
Burley Lawn 9/2103
Burley Lodge 9/2305
Burley Moor 9/2104
Burley New Incl 9/2304
Burley Old Incl 10/2404
Burley Outer Rails Incl 9/2305
Burley Park 9/2103
Burley Street 9/2004
Burnford Bridge 2/2615
Burnshill Common 11/3000
Burnt Axon 9/1902
Burnt Balls 1/1814
Bushy Bratley 5/2208
Busketts Incl 8/3210
Busketts Lawn Incl 7/3110
Busketts Wood 4/3111
Butcher's Corner 2/2615
Butts Lawn 10/2902
Butts Lawn 10/2905

C

Cadman's Pool 3/2212
Cadnam 4/2913
Cadnam Bridge 4/2913
Canterton Green 4/2713
Castle Hill 1/1616
Castle Hill Camp 9/1903
Chilly Hill 1/1713
Church Moor 9/1902
Church Moor 6/2406
Church Place 7/3306
Church Place Incl 8/3309
Clay Ford 7/2707
Clay Hill 9/2302
Clay Hill 4/2811
Clay Hill 7/3007
Clay Hill Bottom 9/2302
Clayhill Heath 7/3005
Clay Pits Bottom 2/2216
Clumber Incl 10/2603
Cockley Hill 1/1915
Cockroad Hill 9/2304
Cole Bridge 6/2707
Coalmeer Lawn 3/2613
Cole's Hole 13/4205
Common Moor 9/2004
Coopers Hill 1/2014
Coppice of Linwood 3/2414
Costicles Incl 7/3210
Costicles Pond 7/3210
Cot Bottom 9/2202
Crab Hat Incl 12/3905
Crabtree Bog 10/2602
Cranes Moor 9/1902
Creek Bottom 9/2302
Crockford Bridge 16/3599
Crockford Green 16/3499
Crockford Stream 16/3698
Crock Hill 3/2114
Crock Hill Green 3/2114
Crow Hill Top 9/1803

Crows Nest Bottom 2/2416
Culverley 12/3604
Cunninger Bottom 1/1916
Custards 7/3008

D

Dames Slough Hill 10/2505
Dames Slough Incl 10/2405
Danes Hole 3/2513
Dark Water 13/4204
Dark Water 13/4201
Dead Buck Hill 1/2012
Dead Man Bottom 1/2017
Dead Man Hill 1/2016
Dead Man Moor 7/2708
Deer Leap Incl 8/3409
Deer Leap Sand Pit 8/3509
Denny Inclosure 7/3206
Denny Lodge Incl 11/3304
Denny Wait 7/3306
Denny Wood 11/3305
Devil's Den 14/2099
Dibden Bottom 12/3806
Dibden Inclosure 12/3906
Dilton 16/3201
Ditch End Bottom 1/1815
Ditch End Brook 1/1815
Dockens Water 5/1810
Dogkennel Bridge 10/2305
Dogsben Gutter 4/2911
Dogwood Bottom 5/2106
Duck Hole 10/2502
Duck Hole Bog 10/2502
Dunces Arch 7/3108
Dur Hill Down 14/1901
Dur Hill Down Incl 14/1901

E

Eagle Oak 6/2506
East Boldre 16/3700
East Copse 12/3705
East End 16/3697
Eastley 14/2498
Eaves Hill 7/3011
Elkham's Grave 15/2598
Emery Down 7/2808
Eyeworth Lodge 3/2214
Eyeworth Pond 3/2214
Eyeworth Wood 2/2215

F

Fair Cross 7/3009

Fawley Ford 12/3804
Fawley Incl 13/4105
Fernycroft 12/3605
Ferny Knap Incl 10/2505
Five Thorns Hill 15/2701
Flash Pond 13/4105
Fletcher's Green 10/2804
Fletcher's Hill 10/2603
Fletcher's Thorn Incl 10/2704
Fletcher's Thorns 10/2804
Fletcher's Water 10/2804
Foldsgate Hill 7/2909
Forest Lodge 14/2198
Foulford 9/1805
Foulford Bottom 9/1805
Foxhill 3/2511
Foxhill 7/3108
Foxhill 8/3608
Fox Hill 7/3009
Foxhill Moor 7/3108
Foxholes 15/2699
Foxhunting Incl 12/3804
Foxlease House 7/2907
Frame Heath Incl 11/3403
Frame Wood 11/3503
Freeworms Hill 3/2212
Fritham 3/2314
Fritham Bridge 3/2114
Fritham Cross 6/2310
Fulliford Bog 8/3408
Fulliford Passage 8/3407
Furzy Brow 11/3505
Furze Hill 11/3201
Furzey Lawn Incl 4/3010
Furzey Lodge 12/3602

G

Gatewood Bridge 13/4301
Gatewood Hill 13/4301
Gaze Hill 1/2013
Goatspen Plain 14/2201
Godshill Inclosure 1/1716
Godshill Ridge 1/1815
Godshill Wood 1/1616
Goldsmith's Hill 10/2904
Gravelly Ford 10/2604
Gravel Pit Hill 1/1816
Great Ashen Bank 15/2699
Great Earley 9/2204
Great Hat 14/2199
Great Huntley Bank 10/2705
Great Linford Incl 5/1807
Great Witch 1/1912
Great Wood 2/2515
Greenberry Bridge 14/2101
Green Bury 10/2402
Greenford 5/1908
Greenford Bottom 5/1908
Green Pond 3/2213
Gritnam 7/2806
Gritnam Holly 7/2806
Gritnam Wood 7/2806
Gurnetfields Furzebrake 12/3704

Gutter Heath 4/3010

Hursthill Incl 10/2805
Hyde Common 1/1712

H

Hag Hill 15/2500
Halfpenny Green 12/3604
Hallickshole Hill 1/2012
Hampton Ridge 1/1813
Handy Cross 5/2007
Handy Cross Plain 5/1907
Hanging Shoot 14/2299
Hardley Roman Road 13/4204
Hart Hill 6/2610
Hart Hill 1/1714
Hart Hill 6/2406
Harvest Slade Bottom 5/2006
Hasley Hill 5/1911
Hasley Hole 1/1812
Hasley Incl 1/1912
Hatchet Gate 16/3701
Hatchet Moor 16/3500
Hatchet Pond 16/3601
Hawk Hill 11/3503
Hawkhill 12/3603
Hawkhill Incl 11/3502
Hazel Hill 4/2911
Hedge Corner 11/3301
High Corner 5/1900
High Coxlease 7/2906
Highland Water 6/2508
Highland Water Incl 6/2409
Hill Top 13/4003
Hincheslea Bog 15/2700
Hincheslea Holms 15/2600
Hincheslea Moor 15/2601
Hiscocks Hill 3/2213
Holidays Hill 6/2607
Holidays Hill Cottage 7/2707
Holidays Hill Incl 6/2607
Holland Bottom 1/1712
Hollands Wood 11/3004
Holly Hatch Cottage 3/2112
Holly Hatch Incl 3/2111
Holmans Bottom 9/2202
Holm Hill 10/2602
Holmhill Bog 15/2601
Holmhill Cottage 6/2408
Holmhill Ford 6/2608
Holmhill Incl 6/2508
Holmsley Airfield 14/2198
Holmsley Bog 14/2201
Holmsley Cottage 14/2299
Holmsley Inclosure 14/2200
Holmsley Lodge 14/2100
Holmsley Ridge 14/2101
Homy Ridge 2/2316
Honey Hill 12/3604
Horsebush Bottom 16/3698
Horseshoe Bottom 15/2600
Horestone Hill 12/4006
Howen Bottom 2/2315
Howen Bushes 3/2314
Hungerford 1/1712
Hurst Hill 10/2805

I

Ipers Bridge 13/4203
Ipley Inclosure 12/3707
Irons Hill 11/3202
Irons Hill 7/3109
Irons Hill Incl 7/3109
Ironshill Lodge 4/3110
Irons Well 3/2214
Islands Thorns Incl 2/2115

J

Jack's Wood 11/3103
James's Hill 7/2808
Janesmoor Plain 3/2413
Janesmoor Pond 3/2413
Judds Hill 2/2616

K

King's Copse 13/4301
King's Copse Incl 13/4201
King's Garden 5/2009
King's Garn Gutter 3/2513
King's Garn Gutter Incl 3/2513
King's Hat 11/3005
King's Hat Incl 12/3805
King's Passage 8/3407
Kingston Great Common 9/1802
Knaves Ash 9/1804
Knightwood 6/2606
Knightwood Incl 10/2506
Knightwood Oak 6/2606

L

Ladycross 11/3302
Latchmore Bottom 1/1812
Latchmore Brook 3/2013
Latchmore Shade 1/1812
Lay Gutter Valley 1/1813
Leaden Hall 1/2015
Levey Hill 4/2812
Linford Bottom 5/1807
Linford Brook 5/1908
Linford Brook 5/2009
Linwood 5/1810
Little Castle Common 9/1904

Little Cockley Plain 1/1911
Little Early 9/2204
Little Eye Green 4/2813
Little Fox Hill 4/2900
Little Holbury 13/4204
Little Holmhill Incl 7/3206
Little Holmsley 14/2100
Little Honey Hill Wood 12/3603
Little Linford Incl 5/1807
Little Witch 1/1912
Little Wood 11/3502
Little Wootton Incl 14/2298
Lodge Heath 11/3302
Lodge Hill 14/2200
Lodge Hill 1/1915
Lodgehill Cottage 7/3109
Lodgehill Incl 7/3209
Longbeech Hill 3/2512
Longbeech Incl 3/2512
Longbottom 1/1813
Long Brook 6/2510
Longcross 2/2515
Longcross Plain 2/2415
Longcross Pond 2/2415
Longdown Incl 8/3508
Longdown Sandpit 8/3608
Longpond 9/1902
Longslade Bottom 15/2600
Longwater Lawn 7/3208
Lord's Oak 2/2617
Lower Canterton 4/2713
Lower Crockford Bottom 16/3598
Lucas Castle 6/2410
Lucy Hill 9/2204
Lugden Bottom 14/1800
Lyndhurst 7/2908
Lyndhurst Hill 7/2808
Lyndhurst Rd Station 8/3310

M

Mallard Wood 7/3109
Mallard Mead 7/3209
Malwood Farm 4/2712
Malwood Lodge 4/2712
Marchwood Incl 12/3807
Margaret's Bottom 2/2615
Mark Ash Wood 6/2407
Markway Bridge 10/2503
Markway Incl 10/2402
Markway Hill 10/2402
Markway Holms 10/2403
Marrowbone Hill 5/1907
Matley Bog 8/3307
Matley Heath 8/3307
Matley Holms 8/3407
Matley Passage 8/3307
Matley Ridge 7/3207
Matley Wood 8/3307
Milkham Bottom 5/2009
Milkham Incl 5/2009
Milking Pound Bottom 15/2998
Millers Ford 1/1816
Millersford Copse 1/1917

Millersford Plantation 1/1917
Mill Lawn 9/2303
Mill Lawn Brook 9/2303
Millyford Bridge 6/2607
Millyford Green 6/2708
Mogshade Hill 6/2309
Moor Corner 16/3201
Moorhill 11/3502
Mount Hill 5/1809
Must Thorns Bottom 1/1914

N

Naked Man 15/2401
National Motor Museum 12/3802
New Copse Incl 11/3202
New Park 10/2904
New Park Incl 10/2905
Nices Hill 5/1911
Nomansland 2/2517
No Man's Walk 6/2506
Norley Incl 16/3498
Norley Wood 16/3597
North Bentley Incl 3/2313
Northerwood Incl 7/2908
Northgate 12/3804
North Oakley Incl 6/2307

O

Oaken Brow 15/2699
Ober Corner 10/2803
Ober Heath 10/2703
Ober Shade 10/2804
Ober Water 10/2702
Ober Water Walks 10/2702
Ocknell Arch 3/2411
Ocknell Incl 3/2411
Ocknell Plain 3/2211
Ocknell Pond 3/2311
Ogden's Purlieu 5/1811
Old House Bottom 9/2205
Old Racecourse Lyndhurst 7/3008
Ossemsley Ford 14/2300
Otterwood Gate 13/4102

P

Park Ground Incl 7/3006
Park Hill 7/3106
Park Hill Incl 11/3205
Park Hill Lawn 7/3106
Park Pale 7/3107
Peaked Hill 16/3699

Peel Hill 8/3508
Penerley Gate 12/3603
Penerley Wood 12/3704
Penny Moor 11/3504
Perrywood Haseley Incl 11/3203
Perrywood Incl 11/3102
Perrywood Ironshill Incl 11/3202
Perrywood Ivy Incl 11/3202
Picket Corner 2/2216
Picket Hill 5/1806
Picket Plain 9/1906
Picket Post 9/1906
Pickets Bury 1/1914
Pig Bush 12/3604
Pigbush Passage 12/3604
Pignal Hill 7/3103
Pignal Hill Incl 11/3103
Pignal Incl 11/3104
Pigsty Hill 9/2102
Pigsty Hill 14/2099
Pilmore Gate 7/2708
Pilley Bailey 16/3398
Pinnick Wood 5/1907
Pipers Copse 4/2713
Pipers Wait 2/2416
Pitchers Knowle 1/2013
Pitts Wood Incl 1/1914
Plummers Water 16/3597
Plain Green 4/3010
Plain Heath 14/2199
Pond Head Incl 7/3001
Pottern Ford 12/3607
Poternsford Bridge 4/3210
Pound Hill 6/2407 & 10/2604
Pound Hill Heath 10/2804
Poundhill Incl 10/2704
Puck Pits Incl 6/2509
Pudding Barrow 11/3301
Puttles Bridge 10/2703

Q

Queen Bower 10/2804
Queen North Wood 3/2313
Queen's Meadow 10/2805

R

Ragged Boys Hill 3/2112
Rakes Brake Bottom 3/2112
Ramnor Incl 11/3104
Ravens Nest Incl 3/2514
Redbridge Hill 7/3109
Red Hill 10/2702
Red Hill Bog 15/2601
Red Open Ford 7/2709
Red Rise 10/2403
Redrise Hill 9/2303
Redrise Shade 10/2403

Red Shoot Plain 5/1808
Red Shoot Wood 5/1808
Rhinefield Lodge 10/2603
Rhinefield Sandys Incl 10/2504
Ridley Green 9/2005
Ridley Plain 5/2006
Ridley Wood 9/2006
Rock Hills 9/2302
Rockram Wood 4/2913
Roe Inclosure 5/1908
Roe Wood Incl 5/2008
Roman Bridge 6/2706
Rookham Bottom 1/1714
Rooks Bridge 9/2303
Round Hill 16/3301
Round Hill 3/2614
Roundeye Hill 12/3607
Rowbarrow Hill 11/3504
Rowbarrow Pond 11/3504
Row Down 13/4302
Row Hill 1/2013
Row Hill 7/3208
Rufus Stone 3/2712
Running Hill 4/2712
Rush Bush 12/3806
Rushbush Pond 12/3806
Rushpole Wood 7/3009
Rushy Flat 2/2117
Rushy Slab 2/2616

S

Salisbury Trench 3/2514
Sandy Ridge 5/2208
Scrape Bottom 14/2301
Seamans Corner 4/2811
Setley Plain 15/2900
Setley Pond 15/3099
Setthorns 15/2600
Setthorns Incl 15/2699
Shappen Bottom 9/2102
Shappen Hill 9/2102
Shatter Ford 11/3405
Shave Green Incl 4/2812
Shave Hat 4/2912
Shave Wood 4/2912
Sheepwash Lawn 15/2599
Shepherds Gutter 2/2615
Shepton Bridge 12/3704
Shepton Water 12/3604
Shirley Holms 15/3098
Shobley Bottom 5/1806
Shoot Wood 9/2303
Slap 9/2002
Slap Bottom 9/2002
Sloden Incl 3/2013
Slufters Bottom 6/2310
Slufters Incl 6/2209
Slufters Pond 6/2209
Soarley Beeches 6/2206
Soarley Bottom 6/2206
South Bentley Incl 3/2312
South Oakley Incl 9/2205
Splash Bridge 5/2011

Sporelake Lawn 11/3004
Spy Holms 9/2302
Stag Brake 10/2403
Stag Park 7/3306
Standing Hat 11/3103
Starpole Pond 12/3805
Stinking Edge Wood 6/2207
Stockley Incl 11/3302
Stockyford Green 6/2606
Stone Quarry Bottom 1/1916
Stoney Cross 3/2611
Stoney Cross Plain 3/2511
Stonyford Pond 13/4103
Stony Moor 14/2199
Stricknage Wood 3/2612
Strodgemoor Bottom 9/1803
Stubby Copse Incl 11/3204
Studley Castle 2/2215
Studley Head 2/2216
Studley Wood 2/2216
Stubbs Wood 12/3603
Sway 15/2898
Swigs Holm 14/2301

T

Tall Trees Walk 10/2605
Tantany Wood 12/3604
The Burrows 9/2302
The Butt 3/2413
The Butts 2/2115
The Hut 9/2203
The Knowles 6/2608
The Noads 12/3905
The Reptillary 6/2607
The Ridge 7/3107
The Weir 15/2801
Thompson's Castle 1/1813
Thorney Hill Holms 14/2000
Thorn Hill 7/3206
Three Beech Bottom 15/2999
Trenley Lawn 15/2801
Turf Croft 9/2005
Turf Hill 9/2102
Turf Hill 1/2017
Turf Hill Incl 1/2017

U

Upper Crockford Bottom 16/3499

V

Vales Moor 9/1904

Vereley Hill 9/1904
Vinney Ridge 10/2505
Vinney Ridge Incl 10/2605

W

Warwick Slade 6/2606
Warwickslade Bridge 6/2606
Warwickslade Cutting 10/2606
Watergreen Bottom 1/2012
Whitebridge Hill 7/3109
Whitefield Hill 14/1800
Whitefield Moor 10/2702
White Hill 5/1807
White Moor 6/2707
White Moor 7/3108
White Moor 7/3208
White Moor 15/2701
White Moor Bottom 9/2104
White Shoot 15/2600
White Shoot 6/2707
White Shoot Bottom 3/2213
Whitley Ridge Lodge 11/3102
Whitley Wood 10/2905
Whitten Bottom 14/2000
Whitten Pond 14/2001
Widden Bottom 15/2899
Wide Lawn 10/2805
Wilverley Incl 14/2401
Wilverley Plain 15/2501
Wilverley Post 10/2402
Wilverley Walks 15/2501
Winding Shoot 6/2406
Windmill Hill 1/1812
Withybed Bottom 6/2510
Withycombe Shade 8/3407
Wood Crates 6/2608
Woodfidley 11/3404
Woodford Bottom 5/1912
Woodgreen 1/1717
Woodside Bottom 2/2517
Woolfield Hill 6/2306
Woolmer Post 2/2117
Wooson's Hill 6/2507
Wooson's Hill Incl 6/2507
Wootton Bridge 15/2499
Wootton Coppice Incl 14/2499
Wormstall Hill 16/3699
Wormstall Wood 16/3498
Wort's Gutter 11/3502

Y

Yew Tree Bottom 15/2500
Yew Tree Heath 8/3606
Yewtree Hill 4/3010
Yolsham Hill 4/2912

New Forest Calendar

ACTIVITY	MALE / FEMALE	SYMBOL		JAN	FEB	MAR	APL	MAY	JUN	JUL	AUG	SEP	OCT	NOV	DEC
Seed Collection		Acorn / Cone	Acorn, Cone	●	●						●	●	●	●	●
Tree Planting		Broadleaves & Conifers	Shovel	●	●	●	●						●	●	●
Pannage		Pigs eat green acorns	Pig									●	●	●	●
Hardwood Felling		Oak & Beech		●	●	●							●	●	●
Hardwood Extraction		Oak & Beech					●	●	●	●	●				
Heath Control		Cut / Burn	Cut, Burn	●	●										
Birds	**Cock** / Hen	Nesting					●	●	●	●	●				
Grey Squirrel Control	**Buck** / Doe	Shoot / Trap					●	●	●	●					
New Forest Ponies	**Stallion** / Mare	Breeding / Sale	Breeding, Sale				●	●	●		●	●	●	●	
Verderer's Court		Open to public		●		●	●		●	●		●		●	
Camping Season		By permit only					●	●	●	●	●	●			
Coarse Fishing	**Cock** / Hen	Season / Spawning	Season, Spawning				●	●	●16					●	●
Brown & Sea Trout Fishing	**Cock** / Hen	Season / Spawning	Season, Spawning		●	●14		●	●	●	●	●			
Wildfowl Shooting	**Drake** / Duck	Season / Nesting	Season, Nesting				●	●	●						●